SpringerBriefs in Health Care Management and Economics

Series Editor

Joseph K. Tan, DeGroote School of Business, McMaster University, Burlington, ON, Canada

SpringerBriefs present concise summaries of cutting-edge research and practical applications across a wide spectrum of fields. Featuring compact volumes of 50 to 125 pages, the series covers a range of content from professional to academic. Typical topics might include:

- A timely report of state-of-the art analytical techniques
- A bridge between new research results, as published in journal articles, and a contextual literature review
- A snapshot of a hot or emerging topic
- An in-depth case study or clinical example
- A presentation of core concepts that students must understand in order to make independent contributions

SpringerBriefs in Health Care Management and Economics showcase emerging theory, empirical research, and practical application in health care, health economics, public health, managed care, operations analysis, information systems, and related fields, from a global author community. Briefs are characterized by fast, global electronic dissemination, standard publishing contracts, standardized manuscript preparation and formatting guidelines, and expedited production schedules.

More information about this series at http://www.springer.com/series/10293

Francesco Schiavone

User Innovation in Healthcare

How Patients and Caregivers React Creatively
to Illness

With Contributions by Cristina M. Thiebaud

 Springer

Francesco Schiavone
Department of Management Studies
and Quantitative Methods
University of Naples Parthenope
Naples, Italy

ISSN 2193-1704   ISSN 2193-1712   (electronic)
SpringerBriefs in Health Care Management and Economics
ISBN 978-3-030-44255-2   ISBN 978-3-030-44256-9   (eBook)
https://doi.org/10.1007/978-3-030-44256-9

This Springer imprint is published by the registered company Springer Nature Switzerland AG.
The registered company address is: Gewerbestrasse 11, 6330 Cham, Switzerland

To Angela and Mario

Preface

Over the last few years, the theory of user innovation became a solid milestone within innovation management studies. Prior studies report that one of the main fields of application of such a phenomenon is healthcare. This industry is currently living a deep revolution for a number of technological, strategic, and social reasons (e.g., digital technologies and big data, value-based strategies and policies, resources allocation and optimization, population aging). These structural changes do not only affect how health institutions and firms design their services offered to patients which are, the final users of most of healthcare products and services. Some of these industry changes also allow many patients to have a more conscious and active approach toward their illnesses and therapies. For instance, nowadays patients use technology to generate and share real-time data about their lifestyles and habits with doctors. Health professionals can better diagnose and treat patients with this information and customize therapies. User innovation, for instance, is showing its potential also during the current Covid-19 crisis. The most emblematic case we have witnessed was probably that of the two-circuit ventilator, a single respirator with two tubes that connect two patients at the same time, created by two Italian doctors to face the sudden shortage of such devices in their healthcare facilities. Another ingenious innovation done by an Italian retired Doctor is the use of a snorkeling mask as a respirator for Covid-19 positive patients with lung complications. All these initiatives clearly show how everyone, by taking advantage of their skills and creativity, can contribute to tackle Covid-19. Only a close and fruitful collaboration between technology and innovators can concretely help our health system to save as many lives as possible from the coronavirus and limit the damage of this terrible pandemic.

Patient innovation is one crucial and inspiring phenomenon within this new proactive approach of user innovation. Literature reports many of them (and/or their close relatives and friends), when they are not comfortable with the existing market offering, they reinvent or create products and services from scratch in order to be able to support and improve their health conditions. Despite the fact that patient innovations form a rising body of literature in both innovation and medical studies, a number of interesting and important research questions are still unexplored: What are the preferred types of new products and services developed by patient innovators? What is the role played by firms, institutions, and health professionals in these processes? Which is the typical profile of these innovators? What are the most common health and economic outcomes, diffusion dynamics, and societal implications? How do digital technologies support the spread of such innovations among patients' communities and within the industry?

I wrote this book for two main reasons. First, I wanted to contribute to this emerging theoretical domain by trying to answer these crucial research questions. "Patient Innovation" aims to explore in detail how patients and caregivers develop and diffuse new products or services and what are the key characteristics of these innovative processes. Second, I wanted to offer tangible bottom-up evidence, solutions, and ideas to improve health systems, organizations, and processes to the communities of practitioners and policy-makers.

The book *User Innovation in Healthcare. How Patients and Caregivers React Creatively to Illness* can be of interest for various audiences. Academic scholars can get inspiration from the findings and illustrations here reported in order to develop and plan new research projects. Students of master programs in both medical sciences and business administration can learn the essentials of this interesting and innovative phenomenon. Health practitioners (such as doctors or hospital managers) can discover the key facts of patient innovation/user innovation and understand how to apply them in their practice. Finally, policy-makers can benefit from reading this book in order to design new regulatory norms and public policies aimed at supporting, for instance, the development and market launch of innovative products and services by patients or the new business creation.

The book is divided in four chapters. Chapter 1 reviews the main literature about the innovative phenomenon of user innovation and develops a taxonomy of the main types of actors promoting it. Chapter 2 illustrates the main research finding and empirical evidence about user innovation in the healthcare sector. Great attention is given to the issues of adoption and diffusion of such innovations within this industry. Chapter 3 focuses on the notion of patient innovation by reporting a detailed literature review and the summary of the main findings. The chapter ends with some theoretical speculations about the potential dimensions to consider in order to develop a proper categorization of the phenomenon. The fourth and last chapter illustrates four successful stories of patient innovation from all around the world. Afterward, the main management, policy, and research implications about the phenomenon are offered to readers.

As usual, I have to thank several people who supported me, either directly or indirectly, in the development of this book. Firstly, I want to express my gratitude to various colleagues (and friends) for their important support in this research project: Luca Dezi, Marco Ferretti and Franco Calza (University Parthenope of Naples, Italy), Eric Von Hippel (Massachusetts Institute of Technology, USA), and Cristina M. Thiebaud, who co-authored with me the third chapter. Secondly, I want to thank my friends Alessandro and Gaetano Cafiero (Kelyon), who greatly helped me to discover the *beauty of healthcare* and to understand how much this world, completely new to me until few years ago, is fascinating and rich of research opportunities. Finally, I want to thank all the students of my course in "Management and Innovation in Health and Social Services" at the Catholic University of the Sacred Heart in Rome (Italy). They greatly supported me in the present research project with their vibrant enthusiasm.

Naples, Italy   Francesco Schiavone
April 2020

Contents

About the Author

Francesco Schiavone is an associate professor in management at University Parthenope, Naples, Italy. He received Ph.D. degree in network economics and knowledge management from the Ca' Foscari University of Venice (Italy) in 2006. He is also an Affiliated Professor in innovation management at Paris School of Business and Visiting Professor at IESEG Business School and the University of Nice (France). He is the scientific director of the research project "Val.Pe.ROC" for the evaluation of the performance of the cancer network of the Region Campania (Italy). In April 2017, Professor Schiavone has been qualified as Full Professor in management by MIUR (Italian Ministry of Education and Research).

Prior research of Professor Schiavone has been published in *IEEE Transactions of Engineering Management, Technological Forecasting and Social Change, Technology Analysis and Strategic Management, Business Process Management Journal, Management Decision, Journal of Knowledge Management, Journal of Intellectual Capital, Journal of Technology Transfer, Journal of Organizational Change Management, Journal of Business and Industrial Marketing*, and *European Journal of Innovation Management*. Currently, his main research areas are technology management, strategic innovation, industrial marketing, and healthcare management and innovation.

Chapter 1
User Innovation

Abstract After a short synthesis of the main key facts about traditional processes of firm-based innovation, the chapter reviews the paradigm of user innovation and illustrates its main characteristics, forms and domains of application. A vast variety of evidences show how this phenomenon is crucial in the support and optimization of innovation in several household sectors. Similarities and differences between user innovation and the new notion of free innovation are also discussed. The chapter ends by proposing a typology of the various types of actors promoting user innovation. They are categorized according to two criteria: the type of user innovator (end-user versus firm-user) and the extent of the innovation process (individual versus collective). The combination of these two dimensions shape four different actors of UI: single end-user innovators, communities of end-user innovators, single firms-user innovators, and networks of firms-user innovators.

Keywords User innovation · Free innovation · End-users · Firm-users

1.1 Classical Perspectives About Product and Service Innovation

Innovation covers a crucial role to support the growth and wealth of people, companies, regions, economic systems and societies. At a firm-level, innovation refers to: "planned changes in a firm's activities with a view to improving the firm's performance" (OECD/Eurostat 2005, p. 34). As the years have passed, economic theory, organization and management studies link the locus of innovation to firms and their activities. Entrepreneurs combine in a creative way the productive factors and resources held by their firms in order to generate wealth and innovation (Schumpeter 1934). Organizational learning theory suggests, the real locus of innovation lies in inter-organizational collaborations (Powell et al. 1996).

Firms can innovate in various domains, such as organizational structure, business processes, technologies and equipment, market contexts, mental models and paradigms of production (Tidd et al. 2005). Product and service innovation relate to the

Table 1.1 New products' categorization by innovativeness

Radical innovation	Innovation that embodies a new technology that results in a new market infrastructure
Really new innovation	A moderately innovative product
Incremental innovation	A product that provides new features, benefits, or improvements to the existing technology in the existing market

Source: Author's elaboration from Garcia and Calantone (2002)

market offering of firms. Product innovation refers to "the development of a new or improved product" (Trott 2013, p. 17). New products and services are some of the main outputs of entrepreneurial processes (Schumpeter 1934). Over the last years, service innovation became a central way to extend the standard set of product characteristics. Thus, product and service innovation are complementary and firms integrate them in designing their offerings in order to gain competitive advantage.

Literature reports several taxonomies of product innovation. For instance, Henderson and Clark (1990) suggest that the combination of two product variables offer different types of innovative products. These variables are the product core concepts (reinforced or overturned) and the linkages between the product core concepts and components (changed or unchanged). These dimensions shape four types of innovative products. Radical innovation refers to new products with changed core concepts and linkages. Incremental innovation occurs when linkages do not change and the core concepts are reinforced. Core concepts do not change but linkages between core concepts and components change in architectural innovation. Finally, core concepts are overturned but linkages do not change in modular innovation. Another taxonomy (Veryzer 1998) considers technological capability (same/advanced) and product capability (same/enhanced) of the new product to categorize four types of innovations: (1) continuous; (2) commercially discontinuous; (3) technologically discontinuous; (4) commercially and technologically discontinuous.

Another way to categorize product and service innovation considers the extent of innovativeness. Garcia and Calantone (2002) offer an extensive review of literature about the main typologies of technological innovation and the concept of innovativeness. The authors develop a useful taxonomy of innovative products (see Table 1.1) by considering three different levels of innovativeness (high, medium and low).

Such definition of radical innovation elucidates also the notion of technology, which refers to "knowledge applied to products or production processes" (Trott 2013, p. 19). Technology offers the knowledge base by which companies develop and commercialize their current and new products (innovations). Technological change is the social and economic process by which an invention becomes a novel technology that diffuses within an industry (Schumpeter 1942). Technological change affects largely market and innovation strategies of firms within an industry. Prior research shows when new technology emerges and diffuses, product innovation is dominant since firms engage competition to impose the new industry dominant design (Utterback and Abernathy 1975). When a new dominant design comes in place, new standards are set up, as well as new designs and technical details. This in term brings attention to new modifications to a base design and therefore makes the competition become creative and more interested in doing further research and development of their products. Once this new dominant design is in market it is stable for a determined period of time until a new one emerges causing a new breakthrough. This can happen over and over again causing a "standard war" (Shapiro and Varian 1999) and in turn having a new dominant design launched when possible.

Organizations can take one of two basic approaches to drive innovation (March 1991). On one side, they can use exploration by investing resources in R&D and trying to find, with basic research, new opportunities and solutions to practical problems. On the other side, firms can opt for the "exploitation of old certainties" and create value from their current knowledge assets.

Literature reports a large number of theoretical models to manage innovation. Scholars recognize at least five generations of innovation models implemented by firms over time (Rothwell 1994):

- Technology-push approach: This is the first and simpler model of innovation development, in which firms sequentially organize the three typical stages of an innovation process: R&D, manufacturing, and marketing. The technology held by the firms is the starting point of the innovation process. Where the output of each phase is the input of the following step.
- Market pull approach: The order of the steps to follow in order to develop an innovation process is inverted. The starting point is the analysis of market needs, then R&D start working in order to develop new products to manufacture afterwards. As well as with the technology-push approach, also the market pull model is linear.
- Coupling: the main feature of this model is the simultaneity of the above-mentioned three stages. Firms adopting the coupling model implement R&D, manufacturing and marketing activities at the same time. Such organization of the process, aims at gaining flexibility and reacting timely to any change coming from the external environment.
- Integrated business processes: firms integrate and develop the phases of the innovation process in a parallel way in order to shorten the time to market of new products. The model works also by the establishment of strong linkages with external suppliers and leading customers.
- Network-based models of innovation: firms tend to outsource to external suppliers some specific phases of the innovation process. Networking with external partners is crucial for companies in order to learn and implement new knowledge.

In addition to the original categorization by Rothwell, a sixth model was coined at the beginning of the present century. Over the last 15 years the so-called open innovation emerged. This paradigm is based on the fact that ongoing development of a firm should ideally include external and internal ideas as well as internal and external paths that lead to the market to make it a stronger and more developed firm. This also gives them the advantage of being more connected to the outside world and

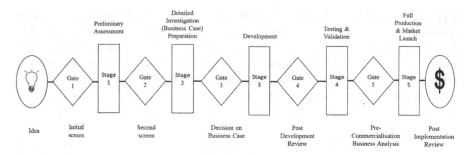

Fig. 1.1 The stage gate model of new product development. Source: Author's elaboration from Cooper (1990)

its needs (Chesbrough 2003). In this last model, innovative firms repeatedly integrate internal and external sources of knowledge during all the stages of new product development.

These models clearly show how the managerial complexity of firms manage and develop innovations, increased over time due to the radical changes in the external environment of firms. Each model considers more actors and sources of information or (revises the order of linkages) than its predecessor.

These models differ in terms of key elements and their linkages. However, they outline quite univocally the structure of a typical process of new product development (the so-called "innovation funnel"). The stage-gate approach (Cooper 1990) outlines five critical phases (Stages), each one followed by a specific check (Gate) to assess the stage output (see Fig. 1.1). In the first stage, firms have to generate a promising business idea to test either alone or with the support of some external partners, via an initial screening (go/kill decision). In the second stage, the idea receives a preliminary assessment that will be reviewed afterwards. If the project passes this second check, then a detailed business analysis is developed. If the project assessment is positive, the development stage starts and, after the post-development review (Gate 4), the stage of testing and validation of the prototype takes place. If the pre-commercialization and further business analysis (Gate 5) provide good market response then the last stage will commence and the official market launch will occur. The high risk of failure for innovation projects throughout the stage-gate process of new product development, often makes the innovator start not one but, in some cases, even hundreds of projects at the same time. Only the best innovation projects will be able to completely go across the innovation funnel.

Firms are the main actors of economic development and promote industry technological change via their innovation activities (Schumpeter 1934). However, the classical firm-centered view of innovation has various limitations. First, firms innovate in order to gain profit. The need of firms to generate revenues limit their interest to explore technological areas or niches that do not seem enough profitable. Producers of goods and services have to develop some specific knowledge about the users' needs and preferences before organizing the product design, manufacturing and commercialization. However, firms usually for several reasons (e.g. time pressure, budget limitations, market size) provide products that just partially match the true preferences of users. The direct consequence of such corporate strategies are several small segments of customers within one market risk to find proper solutions to their needs with extreme difficulty. However, small groups of customers with specific needs can generate valuable revenues streams for firms. The theory of long tail (Anderson 2006) recently remarked this evidence by stressing that small market niches are the new frontiers of business innovation. Nowadays, new technologies (e.g., personalization, co-creation) are reshaping and have segmented many mass markets. Consumer markets are now rich of several small niches, which form their so-called "long tail". Firms can find it much more profitable to focus on these small niches rather than focusing in the largest segments of the market.

The basic assumption of all the theoretical models above mentioned is that the firm is the main actor leading the innovation process; Other actors (e.g., public stakeholders and customers) are marginal players. However, the recent trends in many industries show that products, customers and users are able to lead effectively an entire innovation process alone, without any form of support from incumbent manufacturers. Over the last decades, a shift occurred from producers' innovation mechanisms to collaborative innovation by users (Baldwin and Von Hippel 2011). The remainder of the chapter illustrates the key points of this shift.

1.1.1 The Role of Users in New Product and Service Development

The role of users in the firm-driven process of development of new products and services has been widely researched by both marketing and innovation fields. For many years, marketing scholars have widely analyzed and described the notion of co-creation (Prahalad and Ramaswamy 2004) by which companies can involve the consumers of their services and products in value creation and innovation. Co-creation became a crucial paradigm of value creation for public, private and social enterprises working with various ecosystem stakeholders (Ramaswamy and Ozcan 2001). Literature about inter-firm collaboration in business-to-business markets reports the successful development of major innovations done by small and young high-tech firms and how they depend on the so-called customer mobilization. This concept refers to the "the immediate identification and involvement of customers in NPD", new product development (Coviello and Joseph 2012, p. 98).

Referring to innovation studies, a prior research stresses that users can participate in the innovation activities of companies in many ways (Holt 1988). Beyond user innovation, which is the main topic of the following section, users can be part of two main types of interventions in corporate innovations: (1) user-driven (or centered) innovation and (2) users as collaborators (Gault 2012). In user-driven innovation users promote the corporate innovation process by acting as a source of information. This is the case of the so-called "consumer active paradigm" (CAP) approach of innovation (Von Hippel 1978). In this approach users generate novel ideas for new products and then, they transfer them to firms interested in their development and industrial production. Market research is another traditional method by which firms can collect information and new ideas from users in order to identify the market's unmet needs (Proctor 2005). For instance, the Italian car making company FIAT surveyed more than 3000 customers in order to receive inputs about their cars and to design as best as possible "Punto", a new car model (Kambil et al. 1999). Over the last two decades internet and digital technologies have been offering innovative methods to gain information from users and generate new ideas for new products and solutions. ModCloth, an American online clothing retailer, collects and uses customer feedback to discover the current market trends and to choose the best fashion ideas to implement (King and Lakhani 2013). Both crowdsourcing and open innovation are useful and somehow have complementary approaches that are helpful in collecting ideas and information from users. Crowdsourcing allows a company to reach out to customers in the market and get information about current needs and ideas. When employees were once expected to give this continuous feedback and brainstorm of ideas, this approach is now being directed to the customers; a network of people that invoice their opinions. This is known as an open call (Howe 2006). Open innovation "is the use of purposive inflows and outflows of knowledge to accelerate internal innovation, and expand the markets for external use of innovation, respectively" (Chesbrough 2003)". The primary goal of the first approach is to solve an organizational problem while the key goal of open innovation is to use external knowledge to innovate.

When users act as collaborators of the innovative firm, they actively participate in various phases of corporate innovation (Trott 2013) by providing both intangible (such as information, feedbacks and opinions) and tangible resources (e.g., money, personal time). The active user involvement in product specification, design and development is likely to lead to successful innovation (Rothwell 1986). Alam and Perry (2002) summarize the various forms of contributions made by customers to the new service development of firms (see Table 1.2). These customers' contributions also help with the development of new products. In crowdfunding, the twin phenomenon of crowdsourcing, users actively participate with a firms' new product development by providing funds to the innovation project of a company.

User-firms also act as collaborators in the innovation processes managed and developed by other firms via re-innovation (Rothwell and Gardiner 1985). This approach differs from both incremental innovation and radical innovation. Re-innovation is based on the reinvention or re-adaption of an existing product in the market in the present time or in the past. It uses technology to make these improvements and focuses in doing the proper changes either modifying the manufacturing process, the components or even new designs (Cheng and Shiu 2008, p. 659). A well-known example of re-innovation based on the active role of user-firms is the development of the British hovercraft (Rothwell and Gardiner 1985). Similar situations occur in the construction industry in which various types of user-firms, such as construction firms, real estate owners and generic industry

Table 1.2   Customer's input into the new service development process

	New service development stages	Activities performed by the customer
1.	Strategic planning	Thoughts and feedback on long-term plans (e.g. financial data).
2.	Idea generation	State needs, problems and their solutions, criticize existing service; identify gaps in the market; provide a wish list (service requirements); state new service adoption criteria.
3.	Idea screening	Suggest rough sales guide and market size; suggest desired features, benefits, and attributes; show reactions to the concepts; liking, preferences and purchase intent of all the concepts; help producers in the go/kill decisions.
4.	Business analysis	Limited feedback on financial data, including profitability of the concept, competitors' data.
5.	Formation of cross-functional team	Join top management in selecting team members.
6.	Service design and process system design	Review and jointly develop the blueprints; suggest improvements by identifying fail points; observe the service delivery trial by the firm's personnel.
7.	Personnel training	Observe and participate in the mock service delivery process; suggest improvements.
8.	Service testing and pilot	Participate in a service simulated service delivery process; suggest final improvements and design change.
9.	Test marketing	Provide feedback on the marketing plan; detailed comments on the marketing mix—Suggested improvements.
10.	Commercialization	Adopt the service as a trial; feedback about the overall performance of the service along with the improvements; worth-of-mouth communication with other potential customers.

Source: Alam and Perry (2002)

suppliers, re-innovate existing projects and technologies via virtual reality (Whyte 2003).

Lastly, both end-users and user-firms can support the innovation process of firms by providing a wide range of different inputs. However, in some cases, they can decide to act as independent innovators. This is, without the incentive or support of any organizational partner, as a start-up and leading an innovation process autonomously. This phenomenon is called user innovation (UI).

1.2   User Innovation

Phenomena such as co-creation, re-innovation, open innovation, crowdsourcing and crowdfunding can be complementary in some extent to the broader framework of UI but they just partially illustrate it. In general, a single user innovator is a "single firm or individual that creates an innovation in order to use it" (Gambardella et al. 2017, p. 1452). Literature acknowledges the fact that both end-users (final consumers of

	End-User	Intermediate-User
Individual Process	Single End-User	Single User-Firm
Collective Process	Community of End-Users	Network of User-Firms

Fig. 1.2 Types of user innovations. Source: author's elaboration

goods) and intermediate-users (firms) tend to modify in some extent the way in which they interact with each other and use products. Users have this potential, to revise and re-innovate existing products launched by manufacturing firms and much more.

User innovation is "an innovation driven or created by those who will benefit from using it" (Franke 2013). A single user innovator is a "single firm or individual that creates an innovation in order to use it" (Baldwin and Von Hippel 2011, p. 1402; Gambardella et al. 2017, p. 1452). User innovators can also collaborate and form an ad hoc community in order to achieve their innovation purposes (Bogers et al. 2010). The combination of these two dimensions (the type of user innovator—end-user versus firm-user—and the extent of the innovation process—individual versus collective) creates a typology made out of four possible types of UIs. Figure 1.2 reports the proposed typology.

The acknowledgement in literature of the phenomenon of user innovation is quite old. Spontaneous innovation by users, in the other hand, is not a recent phenomenon. Adam Smith (1776) was the first scholar to observe such orientation to innovation of technology users. This active orientation took place in various forms over the last two centuries. However, the empirical research about user innovators had a surge only over the last 40 years (e.g., Von Hippel 1977, 2005; Rothwell and Gardiner 1985).

Literature reports two main motivations pushing users to innovate (Bogers et al. 2010). The first is the low costs of innovation for users where various elements play part. One of these elements is the stickiness of information held by users. This concept refers to "the incremental expenditure required to transfer that unit from one place to another in a form that can be accessed by a given information seeker" (Franke and Piller 2004, p. 404). The key factor is that it is difficult to transfer information from users to manufacturers. When an innovation process is more manufacturer-driven, it becomes more expensive. This influence in products with high prices is an inspiration for users to develop new solutions that fit their needs and at lower prices. When users have knowledge or training in a specific area that comes handy in the innovation, this also helps decrease innovation costs. Finally, the direct

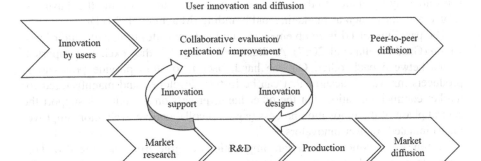

Fig. 1.3 The user and producer innovation and diffusion paradigms. Source: Adapted from Gambardella et al. (2017, p. 1452)

development of innovation by users eliminates agency costs between customers (the principal), which look for new solutions satisfying as best as possible their specific needs, and firms (the agent), which instead are primarily interested in developing innovation at low costs and great profits.

The second motivation of UIs are the expected benefits they can gain from their innovations. UI benefits can be related to personal needs, the willingness to help someone, profit goals, for fun and even for learning (Von Hippel 2017). Within each of these general categories (e.g., personal needs), a large and heterogeneous variety of very specific purposes can be the drivers of user innovation. For instance, users can innovate an old declining technology in order to support their survival within the market and reinforce their technological knowledge and passion. These purposes were found in the radio-amateurs community in which some lead-users developed few multimedia software, freely distributed via internet, to connect old ham radios to the novel and better performing VOIP (Voice Over Internet Protocol) technology (Schiavone 2012).

UIs are not all equal, some users can play a more crucial role than others in the conduction, management and implementation of the user innovation process. This is the case of the so-called lead users which usually have two base characteristics. The first being, they face a need or needs, months or even years before the general market does. Second, they look for a solution to a need they have and therefore have a tangible benefit from it. (Von Hippel 1986). Lead users are the first to perceive the need of some specific product or service within the market and to arrange and coordinate the innovation process necessary to fill in this gap. Lead users hold relevant consumer knowledge, use experience, and innovative personalities (Schreier and Prügl 2008). Firms can apply the lead user method to innovate. For instance, in the construction industry Hilti AG applies this method to innovate pipe-hangers by interviewing and exploiting the creativity of the experts in the topic from 12 client firms (Herstatt and Von Hippel 1992). Lead users can collaborate with firms not only in relation to their innovation processes but also with other business-related activities, such as marketing and branding (Marchi et al. 2011).

The paradigm of UI is complementary (and not opposite) to manufacturer innovation (Gambardella et al. 2017). As illustrated in Fig. 1.3, they exchange important inputs between each other. On one hand, user innovators provide professional producers innovative designs that can be further developed and manufactured for market commercialization. On the other hand, professional producers support the central phase of the innovation process (e.g., via collaborative evaluation, improvement) initiated by user innovators.

A number of policy and welfare implications emerge from the spread of UIs. Users developing their own products (to satisfy their specific needs) balance the traditional manufacturers' tendency to underprovide various products in the market (Henkel and Von Hippel 2004). Thus, the action of user innovators play an important welfare role because they help reduce market inefficiencies. This is why public agencies should support this form of innovation. There are some specific policies that could be useful in achieving this: implementation of more cost-benefit analyses about the outcomes of UIs, promotion of unlicensed use and experimentation of public resources by free innovators and regulatory approaches that are friendlier to these actors (Von Hippel 2017).

UIs can implement the innovation process with or without the support of external actors. As previously described, private firms can support and interact with UIs in various ways (Bogers et al. 2010). UIs are involved in the initial steps of the process, such as the idea generation and preliminary sketch/design of the new product or service. Firms can often effectively collaborate with users like in the manufacturing and operations of the innovation process. Indeed, if these phases entail the production and assembly of physical components, they can be too complex and risky for end-users if not given the support of corporate partners. To this end, companies can offer toolkits to help users design new products. Toolkits are "a design interface that enables trial-and-error experimentation and gives simulated feedback on the outcome" (Franke and Piller 2004, p. 401). Toolkits allow users to communicate their preferred design to manufacturing firms, which will produce the prototype and then give it back to the users (Von Hippel 2005; Hienerth et al. 2014). The watch market is one of the best examples of industries that practice the adoption of toolkits to support the design practices done by end-users (Franke and Piller 2004). Nowadays, the current spread of 3D printing machines is boosting the use of such platforms (De Jong and de Bruijn 2013). Toolkits show that the paradigm of UI is not an opponent but, instead, it is complementary to the traditional firm-centered approaches of innovation.

The latest book by Von Hippel (2017) offers a synthesis of the main surveys currently available about UI. Data comes from six countries (USA, UK, South Korea, Japan, Finland, Canada) and focus only on product innovation. The results show that in the UK there is the highest percentage of consumer innovators (6.1%) in the national population aged over 18. Single individuals develop the largest part of these innovations (83%) in all the surveyed countries. Consumers mainly innovate

Table 1.3 Scope of product development by household sector users in various innovation categories

	UK (%)	Japan (%)	US (%)	Finland (%)	Canada (%)	South Korea (%)
Craft and shop tools	23.0	8.4	12.3	20	22	16.4
Sports and hobby	20.0	7.2	14.9	17	18	17.9
Dwelling-related	16.0	45.8	25.4	20	19	17.9
Gardening-related	11.0	6.0	4.4	Na	Na	Na
Child-related	10.0	6.0	6.1	4	10	10.9
Vehicle-related	8.0	9.6	7.0	11	10	6.5
Pet-related	3.0	2.4	7.0	Na	Na	Na
Medical	2.0	2.4	7.9	7	8	5.5
Computer software	Na	Na	Na	6	11	Na
Food and clothes	Na	Na	Na	12	Na	Na
Other	7.0	12.0	14.9	3	3	23.9

Source: Von Hippel (2017)

products for the household sectors. Table 1.3 reports the detailed information for each sub-sector.

Most of user-generated products and services usually begin their lifecycle as solutions for small niches of market. This makes the individual adoption and market diffusion of these innovations more challenging. The diffusion of innovation is one of the most interesting and well-studied subjects within innovation studies. This process refers to "the process by which an innovation is communicated through certain channels over time among the members of a social system" (Rogers 1995, p. 10). Literature about UI analyzes the issue of diffusion by considering the orientation of user-innovators in sharing (or not) for free their new product or services with other potential users, the creation of new businesses to commercialize the innovations and their adoption by commercial producers (de Jong 2016). Prior research found that there are various conditions that encourage the sharing of innovations done by users, such are: small costs associated with transferring the innovation, pre-existing communications networks in the diffusion of innovation, and the innovators' expectations about the unique value of the innovation for other potential users (Morrison et al. 2000).

Literature reports various interesting cases of UIs developed by lead users over the last decades. These innovations are seen in products, services, business models, new technologies and more. For instance, one of them is the story of Kevin Planck, former American football player and today CEO of Under Armor, a US sport clothing company specialized in the so-called performance apparel segment. Planck's motivation to innovate was his personal need, as reported below:

There was something that, as a senior football player at the University of Maryland I never liked: the way that my cotton t-shirt fit beneath my equipment and wondered why does no one make a better alternative to the cotton t-shirt? I took that fabric to fit the concept I had which was lightweight synthetic stretchy and that could wear snug to the body like a second skin. I took it to a local tailor where I brought him a tight little white Hanes t-shirt and said "Sir, can you make me as many t-shirts that look like this white Hanes t-shirt but out of this fabric?"

Source: "How Was Under Armor Invented? Examples of User Innovation" (YouTube video: https://www.youtube.com/watch?v=5-RS93zKFpk).

This personal need lead Kevin Planck to the development of a new type of sports t-shirt and the creation of its own company in 1996. Currently Under Armor employs more than 10,000 units of personnel, generates more than 3 billion (USD) of revenues per year, and operates all around the world.

UIs can be successful in spreading outside their original market niches and become products for the mass market in the medium-long term. This was the case of mountain bike, invented by some French cyclists in the 1950s. They wanted to ride their bicycles off road but the frames and tires of the existing cycles at the time were too delicate. Thus, solider bikes needed to be made. Years later (in the 1970s), some Californian hobbyists further developed this idea and released the first bikes for mountainous terrain. Another successful example of user innovation is the GoPro. Nick Woodman, an Australian surfer, created this innovative camera in order to shoot selfies of himself when he was riding his surf board. The first prototype of GoPro was simply a camera fixed to the surfer's wrist with a strap. Woodman then created more sophisticated versions (e.g., water-resistant) of the camera, which is now known as the Go Pro and is a mass consumed product worldwide. Users can develop not only successful products but, sometimes, also disruptive technologies, as in the case of the world wide web (WWW). In 1989 Tim Berners-Lee, a software engineer at the Swiss physics lab CERN, created the HTML and HTTP standards to support other scientists from all around the world to work on their collaborative projects remotely. These standards became the foundation for today's Internet, available to everybody for public use since 1993. Finally, innovations by users can contribute to profoundly redesign incumbent industries and spread new economic paradigms. In 2008 Airbnb was started by its co-founders Brian Chesky and Joe Gebbia, who were then only designers living in San Francisco. They decided to rent for short periods of time the free rooms of their apartment to cover daily expenses. After understanding the temporary rent of rooms in houses occupied by others was an appealing solution to many travelers, they started their own business with the support of a third co-worker (Nathan Blecharczyk). Nowadays, Airbnb is a big competitor of the traditional hotel industry.

1.2.1 The Rise of Free Innovation

After 20 years of empirical research, scholars that focus on UI have been able to develop a theoretical novel paradigm that extends the notion of UI and matches it to the most updated mechanisms of diffusion of user-generated innovations. Free innovation (henceforth: FI) refers to the action of customers developing an innovation using their own means without being compensated for doing so. It is also a vulnerable product because no patents or copyrights are implemented so anybody can claim it. Also, while the development and diffusion of such innovation is taking place, no compensation is received, hence the "free innovation" title (Von Hippel 2017, p. 1).

Such definition clearly shows the proximity between free innovation and UI. It's important to note that users lead the innovation process in both cases. Also, a user-generated innovation (e.g., software) corresponds to free innovation only if the innovator distributes it for free. The recent data provided by Von Hippel (2017) reveals patents protect only a very small portion of the UI recognized in the six surveyed countries. The highest percentage protected user innovation is in South Korea (7%). Conversely, in Japan no users protected their innovation. However, the lack of patents does not mean the free distribution of innovation. Thus, Von Hippel and his colleagues asked Finnish and Canadian users specific questions about their personal willingness to give their innovations for free to other users. The results largely confirm such willingness by innovators. In other words, these evidences show that the phenomena of free innovation and UI tend to overlap, at least in terms of size and distribution mechanisms.

Von Hippel (2017) slightly modifies the above reported theoretical framework in Fig. 1.3 (Gambardella et al. 2017) in order to also explain the interactions between the paradigms of producer innovation and free innovation. The interactions with the paradigm of producer innovation are always the same. The key difference is, in the free innovation framework, the starting point is the presence of self-rewarded developers releasing their innovations for free.

Despite the fact that such innovations are distributed without expectations of remuneration, innovators can gain important individual benefits without experiencing specific issues or disadvantages. Prior literature found that they can learn technical knowledge, performance and competencies by collaborating with other innovators or improve their professional reputation, as found in the case of developers of open-source software (Cai and Zhu 2016). The positive consequences of market diffusion are other key motivators that influence IUs to release their innovations at no cost (Harhoff et al. 2003). The lack of economic payment for the consumption of innovation clearly boosts the individual adoption and market diffusion of the new product. Wide diffusion increases the network externalities of the innovation and makes faster and easier product testing and refinements. Moreover, user-generated innovation freely distributed can become an informal standard of the market, technological reference for future innovations.

Literature reports various examples of free innovations. A very rich field of free innovations is the above-mentioned sector of open source software. Communities of open source software developers implement a "private-collective" model of innovation by which "new knowledge is created by private funding and then offered freely to all" (Von Hippel and Von Krogh 2003). A key element of this model is that such free innovations are based on information, which is a non-rival good since it can be shared with everybody without any additional cost. The information-based nature of software, which basically decreases many disadvantages of free distribution, promotes the paradigm of free innovation also outside open-source communities. An interesting evidence is the case of MAME (Multiple Arcade Machine Emulator), an emulation software replicating old arcade videogames from the 1980s and 1990s on modern PCs. This software was not created as an open source but was released by the Italian programmer Nicola Salmoria in February 1997 for free (Schiavone 2014). Ever since, the community of project collaborators periodically upgraded this free innovation and contributed to extend the number of emulated videogames over time. MAME was released as an open-source in March 2016, 19 years after its creation.

1.3   Types of User Innovators

The present section explores in details the four types of UIs reported in the Fig. 1.2. Both scientific literature and professional sources were explored in order to collect specific theoretical information. Evidences and short illustrations about these various actors of UI are also exposed.

1.3.1   Single End-Users

The actors developing such type of UI are individual end-users and/or consumers of an existing product and/or technology to satisfy their personal needs (Bogers et al. 2010). Literature acknowledges some common features to single individuals acting as UIs, such as technical and design capabilities (often exploited via toolkits), and the ability to combine and coordinate their innovation related efforts via digital communication media (Von Hippel 2005). Personal needs or problems are usually the spark of innovation for these individuals. For instance, in his analysis about consumers innovating sport-related products, Lüthje (2004) finds that these people are not interested in profiting from innovation but only in improving their sports experience and performance. The best individual innovators, whose new products are successful in the marketplace, often hold the typical characteristics of lead users and represent the key drivers of democratization of innovation (Von Hippel 2005).

The latest data reported by literature (De Jong 2016; Franke et al. 2016; Von Hippel 2017) highlights this type of user innovation. It is the most common in all the available national studies. For instance, 6.1% of British household product consumers are engaged in user innovation, which means 2.9 million of users aged above 18 (Von Hippel et al. 2012). Available national surveys show that the estimations of consumer innovators in each country are between 3.7 and 6.2% (De Jong 2016). The same surveys summarized by De Jong (2016) also highlight that consumer innovators are less interested than innovative user firms in the protection of their innovation. Therefore, making them more prone to releasing their innovations for free to other users.

We might not be aware but every day we buy and/or use several products and services generated by individual users. The short illustrations of user-generated household products reported in the present paragraph show how technical expertise can greatly help in the development of UIs. However, it is important to note that this resource might not be enough to fully illustrate it. Starting with Slawa Duldig's story, a famous Austrian sculptress, which was uncomfortable with the existing type of umbrella at that time. She thought that it was too heavy and too big to carry around comfortably. Thus, in 1926 she started to think about how to solve this daily life problem. She invented, prototyped and, on September 19th 1929, patented "Flirt", the first folding umbrella in the world. Valerie Gordon-Hunter, a Scottish housewife and mother of six, proves to us that urgent daily needs can boost people's creativity. Indeed, she invented the disposable nappy after the birth of her third son in 1947. Mrs. Gordon and her husband applied for a patent in 1948 and signed an agreement with Robinsons to manufacture the nappies the year later. Their son Nigel was the model for the first diaper. A last interesting case of UI developed within the inventor' house is that of James Dyson's, the first vacuum cleaner. In 1978 he was an industrial designer fed up with the ineffectiveness of his bag-based vacuum cleaner. He took inspiration from his recent work activity and started designing a new type of vacuum cleaner. After 5 years and 5127 failed prototypes Dyson succeeded and patented the so-called cyclonic technology. Now his global company is developing and market-ing household products worldwide. From a technical point of view, these stories prove that both consumers with a specific deep experience and unskilled consumers can develop UIs. Not all the innovators just mentioned respect the two above-reported criteria defining lead users (fast perception of the market potential and expected personal benefits of the innovation). However, all of them had lack of satisfaction for an unmet daily needs with the existing products at the time.

1.3.2 Communities of End-Users

Over the last years, various emerging phenomena in technology and society promote innovation processes and dynamics by communities of end-users. The widespread of ICT and Internet in the past 20 years have facilitated the gathering of people from all around the world on online platforms with common interests on the use of a given product, technology or brand. Three key conditions likely support the rise of an innovative community of end users (Von Hippel 2001): some users have sufficient incentives to innovate, some users are fine with sharing their innovations for free, and the diffusion of the community-generated innovation can compete with the market diffusion of similar commercial products.

The interactions between such people form innovation-oriented communities which are, in some extent, very similar to communities of practice (e.g., Füller et al. 2007). These groups of people have concerns, needs, passions or problems in common and use the internet to find other people with their same approaches. By doing so, they enrichen their knowledge and find support while interacting with others that understand them (Wenger et al. 2002, p. 4). For instance, the existence of virtual communities of old technology nostalgic users (e.g., analogue photographers) promotes the diffusion of the so-called vintage products. New technology-based artefacts aimed at improving the performance of old technology-based products, such as analogue cameras, that became obsolete after technological change have also surged (Schiavone 2014).

The notion of community of UIs also overlaps with the concept of technological niche, which is a "protected space in which these mutations can be tried out and further developed as long as they cannot compete and survive in mainstream markets" (Schot and Geels 2007). Within technological niches, "learning processes are not only about technology but also about the articulation of user preferences and required changes in the government regulation" (Schot and Geels 2007). This perspective suggests the development and diffusion of innovations by technological communities, thus, depend largely on the amount and quality of the social links and interactions between the potential members of the community.

Innovations generated from communities of end-users often overlap, extend and increment the innovation activities of incumbent companies. Industry firms can adopt various strategic reactions to this form of user innovation, which can either compete or complement corporate innovation (De Jong and De Bruijn 2013). Such reactions are: (1) monitor the activity of the user community, (2) attack its activities, (3) adopt the innovations generated by the community, (4) acquire the entire community, and (5) facilitate the innovation processes of the community. Reactions such as adopt and facilitate show that innovative communities of end users can often become important elements of the ecosystem of firms adopting open innovation (King and Lakhani 2013). Literature reports a large amount of evidences of innovative communities of end users. One of the most famous cases illustrated in literature (e.g., Von Hippel 2001) is the community of developers of the Apache open-source software. Since 1995 thousands of users have contributed to the development of this web server software, which is still popular in the market and able to compete with commercial products. A more recent case is the online community of 3D printer users, which collaboratively develop open-source innovations (De Jong and de Bruijn 2013). The power of communities does not relate just to innovation but also to branding. For instance, Füller and von Hippel (2008) found that communities of users can create their own brands without costs. Under given conditions, user-generated brands can become very powerful and be attractive to producers and push for the implementation of co-branding activities. Moreover, firms with strong brands can intentionally exploit the communities' innovative power. Ducati, the Italian manufacturer of motorcycles, created a specific blog and an online brand community to ask for support and feedback from their users to develop new products that adapt to their needs and requests (Marchi et al. 2011).

1.3.3 Single Firm-Users

In this type of UI, an innovative user firm develops a specific technology or equipment that later uses for their own business processes (e.g., manufacturing, information systems management, logistics). Sometimes a user-firm can also be an individual, for instance an architect, innovating a technology or product for professional purposes (Whyte 2003). Von Hippel (2005, p. 3) clearly highlights the difference between producer-innovators and this type of UI with the Boeing example. Boeing is an airplane manufacturer company that can be categorized as an intermediate user. This is because they are innovators in metal-forming machines which they use for their airplanes' assembling, this is known as user-developed innovation or user innovator. They also innovate by designing and assembling unique airplanes, which makes them manufacturer-innovators. Both of the above mentioned makes them intermediate users because they use inputs developed by themselves and incorporate them in their production process (Bogers et al. 2010, p. 857).

Prior research found innovative user-firms in a variety of industries, such as, petroleum processes, machine tools, pipe hanger hardware, commercial banking and many more. In his seminal work about semiconductor industry Von Hippel (1977) found that a key feature of user-firms innovating their process equipment was a large market share. This characteristic is a better predictor for this type of UI than other traditional measures, such as firm size and patenting activities. The presence of national innovation systems also play an important role in stimulating this form of UI. Lee (1996) reports the impressive case of Japanese firms in shaping the innovation dynamics of US machine tools. Between the years 1963 and 1986 the most innovative Japanese firms (such as Toyoda Koki, Sumitomo Electric, Honda Motor, and Toshiba) received hundredths of patent grants in the USA for radical, incremental or small improvements to existing machine tools.

A recent review of ad hoc national surveys about user innovation by firms (De Jong 2016) shows this phenomenon is quite common everywhere and reveals interesting information about this specific type of UI. Data show clear differences between this type of UIs and individual users in relation to the protection and diffusion of innovations. Firms protect their innovations more than end-users (mainly via patents)and are less prone to releasing them for free. In other words, the profit-orientation of single user-firms affects their approach to the openness and diffusion of their innovations.

Scientific literature and professional magazines report various empirical evidences about innovation by single firm-users. Harhoff et al. (2003) provide various examples of innovative user-firms from various industries that benefited from revealing their innovations for free. For instance, in the 1990s IBM developed an innovative process to manufacture semiconductors by incorporating copper interconnections among circuit elements instead of the traditionally-used aluminum ones. This innovative process notoriously improved the semiconductor's performance. Another study about companies in the construction industry shows various types of lead user firms. These are real estate owners and construction contractors, that use virtual reality to innovate, especially on the implementation of large unique projects and small initiatives of design reuse (Whyte 2003). Public non-profit organizations can also belong to this type of UI. In 2017 the Glenn research center by NASA, the US National Aeronautics and Space Administration, developed the so-called Super elastic tire, an innovative alternative to the traditional pneumatic tires. The new NASA tire is made out of shape memory alloys as load bearing components. This material greatly enhances the product performance because it eliminates the risk of puncture and deformation. It also does not need any air or inner frame for the tire/wheel assembly. The NASA research center developed this tire for future Mars missions but its potential applications are several also on Earth. For example in: all-terrain vehicles, military vehicles, aircrafts, etc.

1.3.4 Networks of Firm Users

This type of UI occurs when user firms (or institutions) collaborate to innovate an existing product, service or technology for their specific needs. These innovation networks are horizontal since they are formed by "user/self-manufacturer" firms interconnected by information transfer links (face-to-face, virtual communication and so on) (Von Hippel 2007). This type of UI overlaps in some extent with the concept of open innovation since in both of these cases there are ecosystems of firms tied together by collaborative innovation projects. Networks of innovative user-firms do not develop new products for the market but try to generate new inputs for their production process. Despite the fact that this type of UI is probably one of the less explored by scholars of this specific domain of innovation studies, we can still find some evidence in the literature. A well-known case of this type of UI refers to the modifications to OPAC—Online Public Access Catalog, the leading information search system for libraries—used by 464 Australian libraries, which accommodates to their needs and allows the sharing amongst each other of the revised versions of the original software (Morrison et al. 2000).

Other examples of networks of innovative user-firms can be found in literature about other fields of business and management studies. Wandahl and co-workers (Wandahl et al. 2011) report the case of a Danish supply network generating user-driven innovations in the construction material industry. The "InnoDoor" project, funded by the Danish Enterprise and Construction Authority, supported the development of user innovations from the national industrial network of firms selling components, manufacturing and commercializing doors in Denmark. Successful innovations came out from the effective interplay of user-level and network-level activities and processes. Even the literature about industrial districts, which are regional networks of firms tied by both competitive and collaborative relationships (Marshall 1920), provides various evidences of how such firms can commonly innovate equipment or machineries they use to improve the production process. A well-known example comes from Emilia-Romagna, an Italian region, where over time many small and medium firms working in the ceramics districts of Sassuolo became specialized in the development and production of dedicated innovative industrial machineries (Brusco et al. 1996; Russo 1986). In the industrial districts model, the geographic proximity between local firms supports the spread of information and promotes dynamics of organizational learning. Similar phenomena lead to "collective" user-driven technical change and process innovation, which are key characteristics of such geographic networks of industrial production (Marshall 1920; Varaldo and Ferrucci 1996).

1.4 Conclusions

The present chapter summarizes and offers readers the main theories, concepts, and examples of UI. This paradigm might overlap in some extent with other user-centered phenomena above illustrated, such as crowdsourcing and re-innovation. However, some relevant characteristics of UI make this paradigm more specific and powerful than other paradigms. Such power derives from at least two elements: the diffusion and the welfare impact of the phenomenon. Recent empirical studies show UI as a "mass phenomenon" engaging millions of people all around the world (Franke et al. 2016). The voluntary innovation efforts of users, thus, can lead to important savings for citizens, private companies and national governments.

Prior literature reports different types of user innovators exist. They can be single people or firms that decided to develop new products either alone or in collaboration with someone else. All the various types of UIs (lead users or not) share at least two basic common elements. First, all UIs hold a specific skilled (technical or not) knowledge enabling them to perceive in advance some unmet needs by the market and autonomously develop a specific innovation process. Second, these users suffer from the lack of a specific product that would solve their daily problems or would aid them in their routine activities.

Innovative users can internalize all the steps of the innovation process or outsource some phases to external partners, such as firms requested to manufacture the product physically. However, user innovation is not just a valid extension of the paradigm of producers' innovation. The research findings and evidences reported in this chapter show that these paradigms are not in conflict but are complementary approaches to innovation that can interact effectively.

A variety of audiences should pay attention to how users generate innovations. Scholars should further extend their understanding of the phenomenon and its recent evolutionary trends due to the rise of digital technologies. Moreover, more measurement tools should be developed and provided. Practitioners could explore novel ways, more sophisticated than toolkits, to involve innovative communities of end-users in new product development and their personal projects. Policy-makers should foster UI and promote public policies and programs to strengthen the complementarity between this paradigm and producers' innovations. The reinforcement of the communication channels between companies and innovative users is another key goal.

Finally, previous studies widely recognized the wide spread of the user innovation paradigm in various business segments of the household industry. One of such industries is healthcare. The second chapter of the book completely focuses on the various motivations of the success of UI within the medical and healthcare sector. It also reports a large number of applications of this bottom-down approach of innovation within this context.

References

Alam, I., & Perry, C. (2002). A customer-oriented new service development process. *Journal of Services Marketing, 16*(6), 515–534.

Anderson, C. (2006). *The long tail: Why the future of business is selling less of more*. New York: Hyperion.

Baldwin, C., & Von Hippel, E. (2011). Modeling a paradigm shift: From producer innovation to user and open collaborative innovation. *Organization Science, 22*(6), 1399–1417.

Bogers, M., Afuah, A., & Bastian, B. (2010). Users as innovators: A review, critique, and future research directions. *Journal of Management, 36*(4), 857–875.

Brusco, S., Cainelli, G., Forni, F., Franchi, M., Malusardi, A., & Righetti, R. (1996). The evolution of industrial districts in Emilia-Romagna. *Research Series-International Institute For Labour Studies*, 17–36.

Cai, Y., & Zhu, D. (2016). Reputation in an open source software community: Antecedents and impacts. *Decision Support Systems, 91*, 103–112.

Cheng, C. J., & Shiu, E. C. (2008). Re-innovation: The construct, measurement, and validation. *Technovation, 28*(10), 658–666.

Chesbrough, H. W. (2003). *Open innovation: The new imperative for creating and profiting from technology*. Boston: Harvard Business School Press.

Cooper, R. G. (1990). Stage-gate systems: A new tool for managing new products. *Business Horizons, 33*(3), 44–54.

Coviello, N. E., & Joseph, R. M. (2012). Creating major innovations with customers: Insights from small and young technology firms. *Journal of Marketing, 76*(6), 87–104.

De Jong, J. P. (2016). The empirical scope of user innovation. In D. Harhoff & K. R. Lakhani (Eds.), *Revolutionizing innovation: Users, communities and open innovation*. Cambridge, MA: MIT.

De Jong, J. P., & De Bruijn, E. (2013). Innovation lessons from 3-D printing. *MIT Sloan Management Review, 54*(2), 43.

Franke, N. (2013). User-driven innovation. In M. Dodgson, D. M. Gann, & N. Phillips (Eds.), *Oxford handbook of innovation management*. Oxford, UK: Oxford University Press.

Franke, N., & Piller, F. (2004). Value creation by toolkits for user innovation and design: The case of the watch market. *Journal of Product Innovation Management, 21*(6), 401–415.

Franke, N., Schirg, F., & Reinsberger, K. (2016). The frequency of end-user innovation: A re-estimation of extant findings. *Research Policy, 45*(8), 1684–1689.

Füller, J., & von Hippel, E. (2008). *Costless creation of strong brands by user communities: Implications for producer-owned brands*. Sloan Working Paper, Sloan School of Management, Massachusetts Institute of Technology.

Füller, J., Jawecki, G., & Mühlbacher, H. (2007). Innovation creation by online basketball communities. *Journal of Business Research, 60*(1), 60–71.

Gambardella, A., Raasch, C., & von Hippel, E. (2017). The user innovation paradigm: Impacts on markets and welfare. *Management Science, 63*(5), 1450–1468.

Garcia, R., & Calantone, R. (2002). A critical look at technological innovation typology and innovativeness terminology: A literature review. *Journal of Product Innovation Management, 19*(2), 110–132.

Gault, F. (2012). User innovation and the market. *Science and Public Policy, 39*(1), 118–128.

Harhoff, D., Henkel, J., & Von Hippel, E. (2003). Profiting from voluntary information spillovers: How users benefit by freely revealing their innovations. *Research Policy, 32*(10), 1753–1769.

Henderson, R. M., & Clark, K. B. (1990). Architectural innovation: The reconfiguration of existing product technologies and the failure of established firms. *Administrative Science Quarterly, 35*, 9–30.

Henkel, J., & Von Hippel, E. (2004). Welfare implications of user innovation. *The Journal of Technology Transfer, 30*(1–2), 73–87.

Herstatt, C., & Von Hippel, E. (1992). From experience: Developing new product concepts via the lead user method: A case study in a "low-tech" field. *Journal of Product Innovation Management, 9*(3), 213–221.

Hienerth, C., Lettl, C., & Keinz, P. (2014). Synergies among producer firms, lead users, and user communities: The case of the LEGO producer–user ecosystem. *Journal of Product Innovation Management, 31*(4), 848–866.

Holt, K. (1988). The role of the user in product innovation. *Technovation, 7*(3), 249–258.

Howe, J. (2006). The rise of crowdsourcing. *Wired Magazine, 14*(6), 1–4.

Kambil, A., Friesen, G. B., & Sundaram, A. (1999). Co-creation: A new source of value. *Outlook Magazine, 3*(2), 23–29.

King, A., & Lakhani, K. R. (2013). Using open innovation to identify the best ideas. *MIT Sloan Management Review, 55*(1), 41.

Lee, K. R. (1996). The role of user firms in the innovation of machine tools: The Japanese case. *Research Policy, 25*(4), 491–507.

Lüthje, C. (2004). Characteristics of innovating users in a consumer goods field: An empirical study of sport-related product consumers. *Technovation, 24*(9), 683–695.

March, J. G. (1991). Exploration and exploitation in organizational learning. *Organization Science, 2*(1), 71–87.

Marchi, G., Giachetti, C., & De Gennaro, P. (2011). Extending lead-user theory to online brand communities: The case of the community Ducati. *Technovation, 31*(8), 350–361.

Marshall, A. (1920). *Industry and trade: A study of industrial technique and business organization; and of their influences on the conditions of various classes and nations.* London: Macmillan.

Morrison, P. D., Roberts, J. H., & Von Hippel, E. (2000). Determinants of user innovation and innovation sharing in a local market. *Management Science, 46*(12), 1513–1527.

OECD/Eurostat. (2005). *Oslo manual: Guidelines for collecting and interpreting innovation data* (3rd ed.). Paris: OECD Publishing.

Powell, W. W., Koput, K. W., & Smith-Doerr, L. (1996). Interorganizational collaboration and the locus of innovation: Networks of learning in biotechnology. *Administrative Science Quarterly, 41*, 116–145.

Prahalad, C. K., & Ramaswamy, V. (2004). Co-creation experiences: The next practice in value creation. *Journal of Interactive Marketing, 18*(3), 5–14.

Proctor, T. (2005). *Essentials of marketing research* (4th ed.). Englewood Cliffs, NJ: Prentice-Hall.

Ramaswamy, V., & Ozcan, K. (2001). *The co-creation paradigm.* Stanford, CA: Stanford University Press.

Rogers, E. M. (1995). *Diffusion of innovations.* New York: The Free Press.

Rothwell, R. (1986). Innovation and re-innovation: A role for the user. *Journal of Marketing Management, 2*(2), 109–123.

Rothwell, R. (1994). Towards the fifth-generation innovation process. *International Marketing Review, 11*(1), 7–31.

Rothwell, R., & Gardiner, P. (1985). Invention, innovation, re-innovation and the role of the user: A case study of British hovercraft development. *Technovation, 3*(3), 167–186.

Russo, M. (1986). Technical change and the industrial district: The role of interfirm relations in the growth and transformation of ceramic tile production in Italy. *Research Policy, 14*(6), 329–343.

Schiavone, F. (2012). Resistance to industry technological change in communities of practice: The "ambivalent" case of radio amateurs. *Journal of Organizational Change Management, 25*(6), 784–797.

Schiavone, F. (2014). *Communities of practices and vintage innovation. A strategic reaction to technological change*. Berlin: Springer.

Schot, J., & Geels, F. W. (2007). Niches in evolutionary theories of technical change. *Journal of Evolutionary Economics, 17*(5), 605–622.

Schreier, M., & Prügl, R. (2008). Extending lead-user theory: Antecedents and consequences of consumers' lead userness. *Journal of Product Innovation Management, 25*(4), 331–346.

Schumpeter, J. (1934). *The theory of economic development*. Cambridge, MA: Harvard University Press.

Schumpeter, J. (1942). *Capitalism, socialism, and democracy*. New York: Harper & Row.

Shapiro, C., & Varian, H. R. (1999). *Information rules: A strategic guide to the information economy*. Boston: Harvard Business School Press.

Smith, A. (1776). *An inquiry into the nature and causes of the wealth of nations*. London: Methuen.

Tidd, J., Bessant, J., & Pavitt, K. (2005). *Managing innovation integrating technological, market and organizational change*. Hoboken: Wiley.

Trott, P. (2013). *Innovation management and new product development*. Harlow, Munich: Prentice Hall.

Utterback, J. M., & Abernathy, W. J. (1975). A dynamic model of process and product innovation. *Omega, 3*(6), 639–656.

Varaldo, R., & Ferrucci, L. (1996). The evolutionary nature of the firm within industrial districts. *European Planning Studies, 4*(1), 27–34.

Veryzer, R. W. (1998). Discontinuous innovation and the new product development process. *Journal of Product Innovation Management, 15*(4), 304–321.

Von Hippel, E. (1977). Transferring process equipment innovations from user-innovators to equipment manufacturing firms. *R&D Management, 8*(1), 13–22.

Von Hippel, E. (1978). A customer-active paradigm for industrial product idea generation. *Research Policy, 7*, 240–266.

Von Hippel, E. (1986). Lead users: A source of novel product concepts. *Management Science, 32* (7), 791–805.

Von Hippel, E. (2001). Innovation by user communities: Learning from open-source software. *MIT Sloan Management Review, 42*(4), 82.

Von Hippel, E. (2005). *Democratizing innovation*. Cambridge, MA: MIT press.

Von Hippel, E. (2007). Horizontal innovation networks—By and for users. *Industrial and Corporate Change, 16*(2), 293–315.

Von Hippel, E. (2017). *Free innovation*. Cambridge, MA: MIT Press.

Von Hippel, E., & Krogh, G. V. (2003). Open source software and the "private-collective" innovation model: Issues for organization science. *Organization Science, 14*(2), 209–223.

Von Hippel, E., de Jong, J. P. J., & Flowers, S. (2012). Comparing business and household sector innovation in consumer products: Findings from a representative study in the UK. *Management Science, 58*(9), 1669–1681.

Wandahl, S., Jacobsen, A., Heidemann Lassen, A., Bolvig Poulsen, S., & Sørensen, H. (2011). User-driven innovation in a construction material supply network. *Construction Innovation, 11* (4), 399–415.

Wenger, E., McDermott, R., & Snyder, W. M. (2002). *Cultivating communities of practice* (1st ed.). Watertown, MA: Harvard Business School Press.

Whyte, J. (2003). Innovation and users: Virtual reality in the construction sector. *Construction Management and Economics, 21*(6), 565–572.

Chapter 2
User Innovation in Healthcare

Abstract Healthcare innovation is a complex and heterogeneous domain to which a variety of professional, institutional, and societal actors contribute actively. The present chapter attempts to shed light on this phenomenon in two steps. First, a general overview of the main information, concepts, evidences, data and trends in health innovation. Particular attention is given to the notion of health technology, the current digitalization of the industry and its relevant implications for business models of healthcare organizations. Secondly, the chapter reports the application of the paradigm of user innovation in healthcare. The author illustrates the issues of generation and diffusion of these innovations in health systems. Then, a review of both scientific and professional references is reported to provide a rich set of historical and recent cases of user innovation by doctors, nurses, and other health users.

Keywords Medical innovation · Health technology · Healthcare organizations · Pharmaceutical products · Medical devices · User innovation

2.1 Introduction

Broadly speaking, innovation in healthcare refers to any "new way of helping medical professionals work smarter, faster, better and more cost effectively while providing high quality care" (Thakur et al. 2012, p. 565). Various reasons make healthcare one of the most important and innovative industries of contemporary capitalism. Different kinds of business segments compose this industry: drug manufacturers (including pharmaceuticals and biotechnology), diagnostics and device manufacturers, hospitals, insurance providers, health technology and information providers (Burns 2012; Mahmud and Parkhurst 2007). Such heterogeneity increases the level of complexity of the industry. In addition, over the last two decades many phenomena, such as national health policies, population demographics and diseases chronicity, rapidly and greatly changed the healthcare industry and how organizations within this industry work and create value (Elton and O'Riordan 2016). Another critical element making complex value creation and innovation for these organizations is the current industrial transition to the technology-driven paradigm of "Industry 4.0", which is rapidly redesigning the rules of the game to which they were used to. This paradigm is emerging in all the business sectors and refers to the industrial application of internet of things (IoT) technologies. In general, IoT refers to "the networked interconnection of everyday objects, which are often equipped with ubiquitous intelligence" (Xia et al. 2012). The technologies offering such interconnection between objects can be used for corporate, commercial, consumer and industrial purposes (Gilchrist 2016). Referring to healthcare, the Industry 4.0 paradigm shapes the six key challenges for global industry stakeholders (Deloitte 2018):

- Shaping future workforce;
- Strategic reactions to changes in health policies and complex regulations;
- Engaging with consumers and improving patient experiences;
- Moving from volume-oriented to value-oriented strategies;
- Achievement of positive margins despite the industry uncertainty;
- Exploitation of new technologies, such as apps and other digital technologies, to increase access, reduce costs, and improve care;

These challenges oblige companies to hold a wide set of managerial skills, such as, human resource management, technology management, customer orientation, stakeholders' management, to outline the general goals of the various innovative business models emerging in this industry. Such disruptive external changes and corporate challenges oblige healthcare organizations to have (or to shift to) a suitable cultural orientation in order to adopt and implement as best as possible the innovative routines, resources, processes, and competencies required by the market today.

Within this context of evolution, UI plays an increasingly important role for healthcare systems, stakeholders, and actors. Literature reports a very long tradition of medical professionals, such as doctors or nurses, which were also innovators of their equipment (e.g. Lettl et al. 2006; Tran and Ravaud 2016). As illustrated in the following pages, UI in healthcare can occur both via individual users or in communities of users. This phenomenon is also boosted by new technologies which make it easier for everyone to create new health technologies or the revision of existing ones.

The chapter is split in two main parts. The first part describes the concept of health technology and illustrates the main current trends in healthcare innovation and its managerial implications. The second part reviews the main scientific and professional literature in order to provide evidence and take a snapshot of UI in this industry.

2.2 The Concept of Health Technology

According to the World Health Organization (WHO 2020) a health technology is the application of organized knowledge and skills in the form of devices, medicines, vaccines, procedures and systems developed to solve a health problem and improve quality of lives. A recent classification about technologies for global health (Howitt et al. 2012) outlines three categories: (1) diagnostics and disease monitoring; (2) therapeutics and preventive treatments; (3) medical and surgical procedures. Thus, diagnostics and treatment strategies are normally also considered health technologies.

The broadness of such conceptualization implies that several heterogeneous innovation actors, dynamics and forms have to co-exist within this industry. For instance, the development of new drugs is a type of product innovation, the generation of new protocols for health professionals in order to contrast specific diseases is service innovation, and the introduction of an intensive care unit within a hospital is organizational innovation. The width of this concept implies a variety of scientific and technical competencies that contribute to the development and innovation of health technologies, such as biologics, management, epidemiology, information technology, chemistry, and many more.

The history of health technologies is millenary. The first traces of health technology, as we know it today, come from Egypt where in 2600 BC Imhotep described the diagnosis and treatment of 200 diseases (Hajar 2015). Ever since, the scope of health technology has increased continuously. A critical component of health technology is medical technology, which is "used to ensure health in individuals suffering from a wide range of conditions and is involved in an entire pathway from diagnosis to cure" (Medtech Europe 2014). The scope of medical technology is definitely narrower since it focuses just on two broad categories: medical devices and in vitro diagnostics. Different product groups within the medical technology industry are: imaging devices, non-imaging diagnostics, research and other equipment, therapeutic devices, other services and products. Moreover, medical technology does not comprise some important means by which organizations and professional can provide better care to patients, such as organizational systems and structures.

Throughout the last 20 years, complexity, innovativeness and variety of health technology have been rapidly increasing. Digitalization (as illustrated in detail below) drives the present era of disruptive innovation of health technologies and the current phase of creative destruction of medicine (Topol and Hill 2012). IoT and other digital technologies offer great opportunities to differentiate and improve the value and efficiency of many health products and services.

2.2.1   Health Technology Assessment

Over the last two decades, the assessment of healthcare technologies became a crucial issue for national governments willing to contain health costs and optimize the allocation of resources. Health technology assessment (HTA) is focused on evaluating the impacts of health technologies through a multidisciplinary process. Many aspects are taken into consideration, amongst them there are: social, ethical, economic, medical and many more. Once all of them are evaluated a proper assessment of the effects health technology has can be done and therefore more

Table 2.1 Key principles of HTA programs

N.	Principle
1.	The goal and scope of the HTA should be explicit and relevant to its use
2.	HTA should be an unbiased and transparent exercise
3.	HTA should include all relevant technologies
4.	A clear system for setting priorities for HTA should exist
5.	HTA should incorporate appropriate methods for assessing costs and benefits
6.	HTAs should consider a wide range of evidence and outcomes
7.	A full societal perspective should be considered when undertaking HTAs
8.	HTAs should explicitly characterize uncertainty surrounding estimates
9.	HTAs should consider and address issues of generalizability and transferability
10.	Those conducting HTAs should actively engage all key stakeholder groups
11.	Those undertaking HTAs should actively seek all available data
12.	The implementation of HTA findings needs to be monitored
13.	HTA should be timely
14.	HTA findings need to be communicated appropriately to different decision makers
15.	The link between HTA findings and decision-making processes needs to be transparent and clearly defined

Source: Author's adaption (Drummond et al. 2008)

transparent, patient-oriented health policies can be formulated (EUnetHTA 2007). The need of evaluating health technologies emerged for the first time in the mid-1930s when Bradford Hill, British epidemiologist and statistician, formulated the principles of the randomized controlled clinical trial (RCT) (Banta 2003). Table 2.1 reports various key principles that researchers currently consider in order to effectively implement an HTA program (Drummond et al. 2008).

These principles highlight the fact that HTA is an important driver for medical innovation and technology management. The evidences emerging from HTA report expected benefits, costs and outcomes of health technologies and how these can greatly orient the decisions and practices of institutions, professionals, and companies. National healthcare systems should establish a federal agency in order to supervise and coordinate ad-hoc policies and programs for HTA (Perry and Thamer 1999).

2.3   Innovation in Healthcare

Innovation in healthcare involves a large variety of health stakeholders with specific and different goals: institutions willing to provide the best care services possible, firms willing to gain competitive advantages and profits, patients interested in contrasting their illnesses, and the whole society aiming to improve the national standards of public health. Therefore, medical innovation needs to be an "interactive process involving a broad set of disciplines, agencies and institutions with closer relations emerging between firms, clinicians and academic scientists" (Consoli and Mina 2009).

The development, launch and diffusion of new drugs, medical devices, health services and organizational models are crucial for the creation of value within the health care system. Value in health is commonly defined as "the health outcomes achieved per dollar spent" (Porter 2010, sp. 2477). This definition remarks the close interdependencies for any health (public, private, scientific, institutional) organization between its economic outcomes and the clinical outcomes of patients. Thus, one of the most critical issues for health innovators is to manage the trade-off between these two opposite forces. On one side, health innovators need to continuously develop new and better performing technological solutions to improve the access to care for patients. On the other side, innovators need to make new health technologies that are accessible and affordable to the entire healthcare system (e.g. public payers), which nowadays is much more value-oriented than before. The remainder of the present section illustrates these issues and the main current trends in innovation within this industry.

2.3.1 Patterns of Innovation

A number of researchers in management studies and medical sciences studied the concept of innovation in healthcare. In general, the key characteristics of innovation in medicine are two: (1) new technologies retain a high degree of uncertainty long after their initial adoption, and (2) a close interaction between developers and users is necessary for the development of new medical technologies (Gelijns and Rosenberg 1994). The literature review by Ciani and coworkers (2016) offers a detailed analysis of the main definitions and domains of innovation in health. Medical innovation is a multidimensional process whose main elements are the initiators (supply or demand), the degree of discontinuity with the past (radical or incremental) and the impact (patient benefits, costs, variation in the quality of the healthcare service). Recently, the US research firm Deloitte (2016) listed the top ten innovations in the field of healthcare (see Table 2.2).

Such list of innovative health products, services and solutions prove that healthcare is a very complex industry. A key driver of such complexity is the wide heterogeneity of its industrial and professional players. Institutions and firms from various sectors push innovation in healthcare, (Burns 2012) such as: pharmaceutical sector, biotechnology sector, genomics and proteomics sector, medical device sector, and information technology sector. Each of these sectors hold a specific innovation trait. Complexity of healthcare innovation also depends on the variety of actors collaborating in health companies and forming, all together, the healthcare value-chain (see Fig. 2.1). Such large variety of health actors and sectors highlight the crucial role of technological convergence and managerial capabilities to determine the innovation dynamics and patterns of this industry. Technological convergence refers to the joint use of technologies from multiple sectors. For

Table 2.2 Top 10 innovations in healthcare

N.	Innovation	Description
1.	Next-generation sequencing (NGS)	Applications of genetic sequencing to identify at-risk populations or target therapies to patients who are likely to respond
2.	3D-printed devices	Lower-cost and highly customized medical technology products that can be tailored to suit the physiological needs of individual patients
3.	Immunotherapy	Treatments with the potential to significantly extend survival for cancer patients, without the negative side effects and related health care costs of traditional chemotherapy
4.	Artificial intelligence	The ability of computers to think like and complete tasks currently performed by humans with greater speed, accuracy, and lower resource utilization
5.	Point-of-care (POC) diagnostics	Allow for convenient, timely testing at the point of care (e.g., physician office, ambulance, home, or hospital), resulting in faster, more cohesive patient care
6.	Virtual reality	Simulated environments that could accelerate behavior change in patients in a way that is safer, more convenient, and more accessible
7.	Leveraging social media to improve patient experience	Tapping data from social media and online communities to give health care organizations the ability to track consumer experience and population health trends in real-time
8.	Biosensors and trackers	Technology-enabled activity trackers, monitors, and sensors incorporated into clothing, accessories, and devices that allow consumers and clinicians to easily monitor health
9.	Convenient care	Retail clinics and urgent care centers that provide more convenient and lower-cost care to patients for a number of health issues
10.	Telehealth	A more convenient way for consumers to access and increase self-care while potentially reducing office visits and travel time; may also prevent complications and emergency room visits

Source: Author's adaptation (Deloitte 2016)

instance, pharmaceutical companies could also start selling medical devices by which doctors could monitor patients'(adherence to therapy in real-time). Managerial capabilities refer to the organizational abilities in effectively managing a company in such complex and heterogeneous environments. For instance, technological convergence might push producers of medical devices to implement an acquisition of an IT firm.

Drug innovation also deserves specific attention, pharmaceutical companies are probably the most innovative healthcare actors. Since 1970 the amount of R&D spending grew worldwide at a rate of 12.3% (Munos 2009). Even technological innovation contributes greatly to increase the costs of health care (Bodenheimer

Purchasers	Fiscal intermediaries	Providers	Product intermediaries	Producers
Government Employers Individuals Employer coalitions	Insurers HMOs Pharmacy benefit managers	Hospitals Physicians Integrated delivery networks Pharmacies	Wholesalers Mail order distributors Group purchasing organizations	Pharmaceutical & biotechnology manufacturers Medical device makers Medical suppliers Information technology firms

Fig. 2.1 The U.S. Healthcare value chain. Source: Author adaptation from Burns (2012)

2005). The continuous need of pharmaceutical companies to improve the innovativeness and positive impacts of new drugs also depends on the sterner recent policies for the public procurement of medicines. When referring to healthcare products, such as drugs or devices, many actors are involved in the purchasing of them. For instance, end consumers such as patients and caregivers can acquire them "out-of-pocket" (in cash). In several national healthcare systems, public institutions tend to serve as intermediate-users. For instance, hospitals purchase innovative drugs and medical equipment directly from manufacturers in order to provide care services to patients. Public stakeholders pay for these innovations and decide which health technologies must be purchased (and which not) to supply hospitals and other public organizational units for health assistance. Public payors, thus, pay a lot of attention to drugs innovativeness and their impact on patients and, very often, promote measurement systems to evaluate innovations. For instance, in Italy AIFA (Agenzia Italiana del Farmaco) recently pointed out three criteria innovative drugs need to have, in order to be considered so (AIFA 2017): (1) therapeutic need; (2) added therapeutic value; (3) robustness of evidences and clinical trials. Such criteria oblige companies to perform risky, complex and radical innovation processes in order to be competitive and incentive national Governments to prefer their new drugs.

During the past years the digital transformation of healthcare, briefly illustrated in the next pages, has promoted extensive organizational, service and process innovation done by health companies. Another emerging innovation trend in healthcare, by which organizations are able to implement bottom-up organizational, business and process changes, is design thinking. This method is focused on integrating customer's needs into a designer's product design, giving the innovation a human approach. Technology can also play part giving it an added value and more chances for success in the market. In healthcare, design thinking is often adopted to revise or create new solutions for patients, caregivers and health professionals by listening to their needs and daily experiences with the health services. For instance, the Rotterdam Eye Hospital recently used this approach. Via design thinking managers redesigned the organizational processes, changed the internal environment and increased the customer satisfaction of patients of the Dutch hospital (Deichmann and van der Heijde 2016).

Continuous innovation and open innovation are other current innovation trends of this industry. Continuous innovation not only refers to a product or service but also to the continuous improvement of the technologies used, the management, the processes and even the organization of a firm (Boer and Gertsen 2003, p. 806). Paulus and coworkers (2008) report the case of the Geisinger Health System (GHS), based in Pennsylvania, USA. GHS implemented continuous innovation to develop various new patient-oriented technological services and products. These new services and products are done in accordance with innovation trends in the healthcare industry. Digital technology, described in the next subsection, is one of the core elements of such orientation. Open innovation (Chesbrough 2003) also became very common in the pharmaceutical industry. Merck was a drug producer pioneer which adopted this approach to provide more customer-oriented and cost-effective products via external collaborations for innovation (Horbaczewski and Rothaermel 2012).

2.3.2   The Digitalization of Healthcare

Industry digitalization affected the models of business and innovation processes of all types of health care actors. Technology-enabled care can support healthcare organizations and institutions in reducing costs, increasing access and improving outcomes (Deloitte 2018). Digital technologies are the core element of interactive health technologies, which are defined as "the interaction of an individual—consumer, patient, caregiver, or professional—with a computerized technology to access, monitor, share, or transmit health information" (Robinson et al. 1998). A typical example of interactive health technologies is, for instance, an internet-based information and support system for the following of a patient's recovering. These technologies are used extensively in design thinking for implementing user-centered solutions for patients and caregivers (De Vito Dabbs et al. 2009). The "hype cycle" model introduced 25 years ago by Gartner (Fenn 1995) is a useful framework that offers a snapshot of the adoption, maturity and social application of the main technologies within one industry. The model by Gartner, (American company specialized in research and consulting), outlines 6 key stages of these processes:

1. Technology trigger: events or breakthroughs generating publicity and industry interest in a new technology;
2. On the rise: Media coverage and the interest for new technology by venture capitalists increase.
3. At the peak: the number of companies selling the new technology increases;
4. Sliding into the Trough: sales are less than companies' expectations and some companies exit from the market.
5. Climbing the Slope: Firms work more on the technology to understand better its real impact and implications and revise it.

6. Entering the Plateau: the mainstream adoption of the technology and the real-life cycle of the technology start.

Figure 2.2 shows the latest available hype cycle chart reported by Deloitte (2015) about digital technologies in healthcare. The hype cycle model stresses healthcare is an important field of application also for IoT. Interesting examples of interconnected objects in health are the two robots Giraff and Baymax. The first one was launched in 2013 in Scotland in order to be able to monitor the health conditions of patients suffering of dementia when they are at their own houses by remote control. Baymax, is a robot, developed by the MIT Media lab, with a soft synthetic skin that can detect medical conditions of children (Gilchrist 2016).

The hype cycle model clearly shows the large extent of digital technologies by which nowadays providers of health services can offer e-health solutions to customers. This concept refers to all the "health services and information delivered or enhanced through the Internet and related technologies" (Eysenbach 2001). The widespread use of smartphones in people's daily lives also boosted the rise of mobile health (or mHealth), a new market and technological niche within the e-health sector. The Global Observatory for eHealth (GOe) defines mobile health as the use of devices such as: mobile phones, personal digital assistants (PDAs) and any other related devices that use medical and public health backgrounds in order for them to properly function.

The various dimensions of mHealth reported in Table 2.3 hold different levels of technological complexity. However, all of them are crucial for healthcare organizations in order to collect patient-generated data, which is probably the most valuable, innovative and promising source of health data achievable via digital technologies. mHealth devices and other wearable health technologies are crucial innovative means for the data collection of real-world data by which evidence-based medicine can take place.

An interesting case of integrated m-Health is Tirnet, which is a web-based platform that simplifies access for endocrinologists, surgeons and pathologists to both molecular test results and cytological diagnosis of patients affected by thyroid nodules. Conceived by the Department of Public Health at the University of Naples Federico II, funded by the Campania Region in Italy and developed by Kelyon. The Tirnet web platform represents a good example of a link app between integrated healthcare systems, namely, a technology linking patients with healthcare professionals. In 2017, 15,300 new thyroid cancer cases were detected in Italy and with reference to cancer detection techniques, the thyroid ultrasound screening led to an increasing identification of thyroid nodules, many of them, benign in nature. Usually, thyroid fine-needle aspiration is able to correctly diagnose the majority of thyroid nodules, but up to 30% of thyroid FNA is classified as cytologically "indeterminate", causing unnecessary surgical interventions. Thus, in order to accurately stratify the risk of indeterminate thyroid nodules, molecular tests performed on thyroid FNA may reduce the number of unnecessary thyroidectomies, resulting in a more tailored management of these patients and in a reduction of healthcare system costs. Since regional community hospitals within suburban areas may not have the

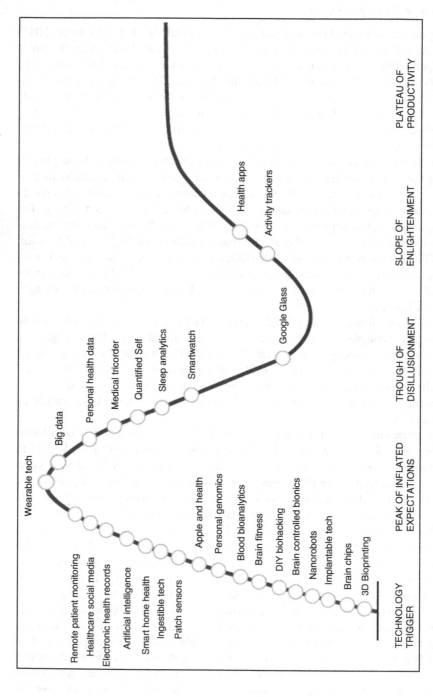

Fig. 2.2 The 2014 Hype cycle of digital health technologies. Source: Author adaptation from Deloitte (2015). https://www2.deloitte.com/content/dam/Deloitte/uk/Documents/life-sciences-health-care/deloitte-uk-connected-health.pdf

Table 2.3 Dimensions of effective mHealth

Dimension	Goal	Examples/Features
Single use mHealth	Focuses on a single purpose for a single user, typically consumer initiated	Smartphone apps and wearable tech products supporting the user to record data which may be communicated to others; consumer driven, focus on wellness, diet and exercise.
Social mHealth	Draws upon the support and encouragement provided through social networks	Gamification and competition-based apps which encourage users to meet goals; consumers likely to pursue activities independently.
Integrated mHealth	Links app and devices with the formal healthcare system	Mobile technology linking patients and healthcare professionals; tailored to multiple end users, consumers, physicians and administrators.
Complex mHealth	Leverages advanced, integrated analytics for decision support.	Predictive analytics applied to complex data generated through mHealth applications; focus on achieving optimal management of a specific disease.

Source: author's adaptation (Deloitte 2015)

right skills or infrastructures to carry out these types of molecular assays, these latter can be centralized to Molecular Biology Laboratories experienced in molecular biology tests performed on cytopathology specimens. Tirnet, based on a hub & spoke model, connects endocrinologists, endocrine surgeons and pathologists, who work in different hospital institutions (Spoke), to a central laboratory (Hub) facilitating them to request a molecular diagnostic test performed on thyroid cells, speeding up the results access process, compared to the traditional way. During the first 2 years of this project, over n = 1000 patients were managed. The Molecular Biology Laboratory of the Department of Public Health, at the University of Naples Federico II (Hub) and seven community hospitals (Spoke) of the Campania Region (Istituto Nazionale Tumori IRRCCS Fondazione G. Pascale, Azienda Ospedaliera dei Colli, A.O.S.G.Moscati, Ospedale Antonio Cardarelli, Azienda Ospedaliera Universitaria Luigi Vanvitelli, ASL Napoli 1, Azienda Ospedaliera Universitaria Federico II) are the partners involved in this project.

The adoption of digital technologies in healthcare augment the need for the organization of holding and management effectively reliable information systems (Wager et al. 2017). For instance, they are crucial to implement approaches, such as total quality management or business process reengineering, that consistently support lean thinking in healthcare (Furterer 2014).

2.3.3 · Implications for the Business Models of Healthcare Organizations

The digitalization of almost all services and products is the main driver for building or revising business models of healthcare institutions. A business model more precisely can be defined as the use of different model units as a base to produce a more consumer oriented organization (Demil and Lecocq 2010, p. 227). The key elements of any business model are the profit formula, key processes and resources, and the value proposition of the organization (Hwang and Christensen 2008).

In general, digital technologies support healthcare organizations in the implementation of the long-tail approach for value creation (Anderson 2007) by promoting the business models built around the "less-is-more" principle. This approach consists on offering more value to customers in minor market niches. These niches are populated by customers having very specific needs which are usually not as appealing to companies, as the mass market is.

As reported by Elton and O'Riordan (2016), four innovative business models for healthcare organizations are currently reshaping the industry. Technology and innovation play a crucial role for all of them. The first and simplest model is the approach of lean innovators, which are product-centric businesses focusing on innovation but with conservative approaches on research and development (R&D). These companies develop and commercialize simple products, such as drugs or treatments to cure specific conditions of patients, in therapeutic areas. Another key element of this model is the strong orientation for corporate acquisitions. The Israeli pharmaceutical company Teva is an example of a lean innovator. The second innovative business model is the so-called "Around-the-Patient Innovator", mainly adopted by large and established drug companies, implementing innovative line extensions of their traditional business. These firms are both science-based and service-oriented and aim to provide solutions for impactful diseases. To this end, they establish critical partnerships with other companies offering technological and digital competencies. A typical example of pharmaceutical company implementing this model is Johnson and Johnson. The third business model is the value innovator approach. Companies adopting this model offer pure personal and digital services (such as integrated analytics) to their customers, which are usually health authorities, risk-bearing health systems, and private payers. The key priority of these innovative health companies is value creation, for instance, by selling services for population, health management or developing system solutions. Finally, the fourth and last innovative approach relates to the so-called new health digitals, which are focused almost exclusively in the value proposition and creation on the adoption and exploitation of digital health technologies. All these business models offer different levels of value and delivered services offered to patients, which are summarized in the "Value Curve" model (see Fig. 2.3).

The effective implementation of innovative business models in healthcare relies on four key challenges faced by health organizations (Hwang and Christensen 2008). First, the fragmentation of the care process between stakeholders is crucial,

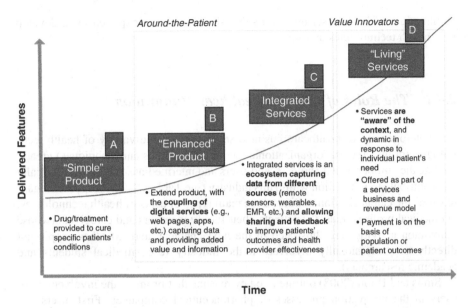

Fig. 2.3 The Value Curve construct. Source: Author' adaptation from Elton and O'Riordan (2016)

this is to create and offer effective value to customers. The adoption of reliable information systems for sharing information and data about patients across health operators is also key. The lack of a retail market in healthcare, which is an industry dominated by the third-party payer system, is a structural condition of the industry hampering disruptive innovation. This lack inevitably limits, in some extent, the orientation of health organizations for business model innovation. Other key challenges for business model innovation in healthcare are the regulatory barriers. Despite the fact that policy-makers often define regulations with initial good purposes, the outcome very often is an increase of costs for healthcare organizations, which, could become less likely to start-up and implement new added-value activities. Finally, the global trend by payer systems in cutting reimbursement for drugs and medical devices make it more complex for healthcare institutions (e.g., hospitals and physicians) to fulfil their value proposition and provide added-value services.

2.4   User Innovation in Healthcare

The effective use of health and medical technology is possible thanks to the expertise and knowledge of people on the matter. Thus, the analysis of users in healthcare is crucial in order to understand the innovation dynamics within this industry. Health professionals (e.g., physicians, nurses, and other medical staff) very often act as single user innovators. The remainder of this subsections provides evidences of communities of health user innovators that share ideas and experiences to develop new health technologies and services.

2.4.1 The Roles of Users in Healthcare Innovation

The heterogeneity of healthcare business segments and the variety of health technologies (drugs, devices, organizational models, procedures and techniques) greatly enlarge the number of stakeholders, end-users and intermediate-users that potentially can contribute to innovation within this industry (see Table 2.4). With specific regard to users, the categorization outlines three main types of users of health technologies: (1) medical professionals, (2) patients, their family members and caregivers (whose innovation activities are illustrated in the next chapter), and (3) other people not directly or professionally involved in the industry (e.g., medical students and academic researchers).

Smits and Boon (2008) outline five key reasons that promote the involvement of users in the innovation processes of pharmaceutical companies. First, users can stimulate the R&D activities of pharmaceutical firms in some specific therapeutic areas that might be poorly unexplored without any external intervention (e.g., orphan drugs). Second, users can offer their experience and knowledge to firms in order to enhance and improve their innovation processes. Third, patients and public actors can make more cost-effective pharmaceutical R&D by promoting fundraising campaigns. Fourth, associations of users, such as medical association groups, pro-life organizations or animal rights groups, can facilitate or hamper the introduction of new health technologies and make their impact on society more transparent. Finally, users have the moral right to influence, in some extent, drug innovations.

The modalities and extent of users' involvement in the innovation processes of healthcare organizations changes largely across health business segments. For

Table 2.4 Health stakeholders involved in the innovative process

Users	Other stakeholders
Medical professionals (general practitioners; specialists—e.g. surgeons, anesthetists—; allied health professionals—e.g. nurses—; professional societies)	Manufacturers
Patients (individuals; patients organizations)	Vendors/distributors
Family members	International regulators
Caregivers	National/domestic regulators
Academic researchers	Health ministry
Biomedical engineers	
Medical students	
Biomedical engineering students	

Source: Adaptation from WHO (2010)

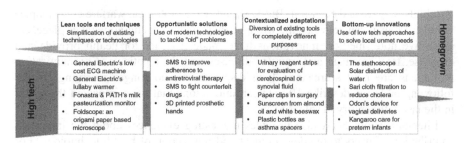

Lean tools and techniques Simplification of existing techniques or technologies	Opportunistic solutions Use of modern technologies to tackle "old" problems	Contextualized adaptations Diversion of existing tools for completely different purposes	Bottom-up innovations Use of low tech approaches to solve local unmet needs

• General Electric's low
  cost ECG machine
• General Electric's
  lullaby warmer
• Fonastra & PATH's milk
  pasteurization monitor
• Foldscope: an
  origami paper based
  microscope
	• SMS to improve
	  adherence to
	  antiretroviral therapy
	• SMS to fight counterfeit
	  drugs
	• 3D printed prosthetic
	  hands
		• Urinary reagent strips
		  for evaluation of
		  cerebrospinal or
		  synovial fluid
		• Paper clips in surgery
		• Sunscreen from almond
		  oil and white beeswax
		• Plastic bottles as
		  asthma spacers
			• The stethoscope
			• Solar disinfection of
			  water
			• Sari cloth filtration to
			  reduce cholera
			• Odon's device for
			  vaginal deliveries
			• Kangaroo care for
			  preterm infants

Fig. 2.4 Examples of frugal innovations in healthcare. Source: Adaptation from Tran and Ravaud (2016)

instance, pharmaceutical companies could mainly benefit from the collaboration of patients for the implementation of randomized controlled trials (RCTs) to test new drugs. Conversely, medical companies producing health devices could offer more active roles to users (e.g., co-design) inside their innovation projects.

User innovation can overlap frugal innovation, which refers to "responding to severe resource constraints with products having extreme cost advantages compared to existing solutions" (Zeschky et al. 2011, p. 39). In healthcare, as illustrated in the remainder of the chapter, users often develop frugal, low-tech innovations. They, usually, are contextualized adaptations of existing approaches and devices or bottom-up innovations to solve local and/or personal unmet needs, as shown in the Fig. 2.4 (Tran and Ravaud 2016).

The practice of medical technology promotes a social control according to Timmermans and Berg (Timmermans and Berg 2003). Some can argue that technology has come to cause negative effects on our lives more than it has benefited us. The truth is, although there have been many negative effects due to the introduction of technology such as: less human work jobs, less emotional and sensitive approach to work, less interaction amongst humans, computerized control of information and many more, there are many positive aspects to this introduction. Strong technological determinists argue that technology develops as the result of an internal dynamic; molding society to fit its logical patterns (Timmermans and Berg 2003). In his work, Timmermans highlights how this molding in society can encourage specific medical innovations to emerge. Such as: In Vitro Fertilization which as stated by Denny "In radical feminist ideology women's desire for children is fueled by pro-natalist ideology and exploited by men eager to master nature", DNA technologies for political uses and more.

Technological advances and its introduction into our social world have greatly impacted the way we move around, communicate and do things on a daily basis. It is undeniable that technology has come to facilitate our lives, to make it more practical and in a way more effective. However, it is important to be able to discern why such technologies have come into play, their purpose and the benefits it brings to our lives. Every new innovation has an interest besides it, the goal should be to better our lives without affecting others and without compromising our health in an overall sense. Technology advancements put in the wrong hands can bring instability, unease and even war. Bio-weapons and a biological warfare are examples of how serious it can get when the wrong management of technology takes place. On a positive note, medical innovations have made it easier for health providers to diagnose, treat, manage and monitor diseases and their patients. Communication limitations are now scarce and long distances are no longer worrying. In the following table we describe 10 medical innovations that have impacted the world in the last half century (Table 2.5).

Literature about HTA also provides interesting evidences about the important contribution of users to the development and innovation of health technology. For instance, the study by McGregor and Brophy (2005) shows the involvement of a hospital technical staff unit in the development of HTA programs and how the adoption of new technology had a great impact on this. The unit consisted of administration members, health-care professionals, patients, and representatives of clinical disciplines. It seems more fruitful to let the users in the health care sector to participate in parts of the process, instead of making the users lead the process (Røtnes and Dybvik Staalesen 2010). This is because if they are seen as lead users more burden is put on them which adds more pressure to their ailment. Not all innovations are done to cure or treat a disease, some are done to make life easier or to better cope with an illness. This is why the insight of the patient is very important in the innovation process.

2.4.2   Evidences of User Innovation in Healthcare

Literature widely acknowledges the crucial and active role of doctors and other health care professionals in health innovation. Physicians have been long recognized as the most active and prolific category of health user innovators. The history of medicine shows that doctors can also innovate without firms successfully. Literature reports several cases of ancient doctor-generated innovations. A well-known example of user-generated health innovation is the stethoscope, invented by the French doctor Renè Laennec (1781–1826) more than two centuries ago. Fayssoil (2009, p. 744) precisely reports:

> In September 1816, in the Louvre's gardens, he observed 2 children who were playing with a long piece of solid wood and a pin. With an ear to one end, a child heard an amplified sound of the pin scratching the opposite end of the wood. The same year, called to examine a young woman but embarrassed because of her age, gender, and corpulence, Laennec used a sheaf of paper rolled into a cylinder to auscultate the heart. By applying one end of the cylinder to her chest and the other to his ear, he heard clear amplified sounds as he had never been able to hear before. The stethoscope was invented!

Shaw (1985) states that when healthcare providers collaborate with professional manufacturers, they become leading innovators in several sub-areas of the medical equipment industry. The continuous and stable interactions between doctors and firms in these user dominated innovation processes occur very frequently in the evaluation, development of prototypes, product specification and marketing. Doctors

Table 2.5 The 10 Greatest medical inventions of the last 50 years

Invention	Characteristics
Magnetic resonance imaging (MRI) and computerized tomography (CT)	Two widely used medical technologies nowadays. The first whole-body MRI scanner was assembled in 1977 by Dr. Damadian. CT scans were created by sir Godfrey Hounsfield and Dr. Alan Cormack (innovation for which they were awarded a Nobel prize in 1979).
The artificial heart	Currently, temporary and permanent artificial hearts are being used to help patients stay healthy while awaiting a heart transplant or to nurse their current hearts back to health. Inventor: Robert, Jarvik, MD.
Laser surgeries	Usually used for corrective eye surgeries, cosmetic dermatology and many more medical procedures. Light amplification by stimulated emission of radiation (LASER) allows a more detailed and precise approach to very small areas of the body.
Minimally invasive robotic surgeries	Robots that aid in minimally invasive surgeries (Ex. the "Da Vinci" robot). These minimally-invasive surgeries leave a few small marks on the body and allow for greater accuracy during surgery and less post-operation recovery time.
Functional magnetic resonance imaging (fMRI)	This non-invasive technology records signals, blood flow and activity areas in the brain. It can also be used to follow-up brain tumors and diagnose abnormalities. Its advantage is that it doesn't cause radiation.
Highly active anti-retroviral therapy (HAART)	Using three medications to create one powerful combination
Modern Telehealth	This focus allows doctors and patients to connect with each other through the use of online platforms. Through this online communication better diagnosis, treatment and care management can be provided to patients. A proper availability of their medical records and imaging is also possible.
Molecular breast imaging (MBI)	While mammography has been one of leading methods of detection for breast cancer for years, it has not been effective in detecting tumors in dense tissue. MBI is a safe and more powerful scan which serves as an encouraging alternative to mammography.
Health IT (especially Mobile/wireless devices)	Useful for Looking up information, accessing patient records, and viewing digital medical information in seconds.
Active bionic prosthesis (wearable robotic devices)	These medical innovations help replace and replicate human extremities. Some are even enabled by Bluetooth, motors and even microprocessors.

Source: Adaptation from Healthcare Business & Technology

Table 2.6 Cases of user-generated techniques in surgery

N:	Surgical field	Area of application	Technique	User innovator (Year)
1.	Hand surgery	Peripheral nerve Surgery	Endoscopic approach to treat a nerve compression syndrome	Hand surgeon (2004)
2.	Neurosurgery	Brain surgery	Endoscopic approach to treat a neuro condition	Neurosurgeon (1990s)
3.	HNO/NOS	Endocrinology	Minimally-invasive approach to the thyroid gland	ENT (ear, nose and throat) surgeon (2005–2009)
4.	NOTES (Natural orifice transluminal endo-scopic surgery)	Hand surgery	Transvaginal cholecystectomy	General surgeon (2007)

Source: Adaptation from Hinsch et al. (2014)

provide critical information and networking to industrial partners and can participate in the radical innovation process as inventors, entrepreneurs and developers or co-developers (Lettl et al. 2006).

Academic literature in both innovation studies and medical reports, state that surgeons are definitely the most active community of health professionals in the practice and device innovation among the various medical specializations (Lettl et al. 2006; Riskin et al. 2006; Hinsch et al. 2014). Referring to medical practices, a recent article by Hinsch and co-workers (2014) shows that surgery is a medical domain in which user innovation in techniques is very common (see Table 2.6). German surgeons developed all the illustrated techniques, which were able to both enhance the functional value of existing products and stimulate new product development by users and manufacturers.

The story about the development of the new technique for hand surgery is very interesting. The innovative doctor used his prior experience in hand surgery to generate a minimally invasive technique. In 2004, with the support of a nurse, he started to use instruments from other surgical fields to identify and design this new procedure. Moreover, the surgeon approached a product manufacturer to create a specific instrument to further develop his new technique. Finally, he directly promoted his new technique among colleagues via conferences calls, workshops and seminars. In 2008 this practice became the recommended approach by the main association of specialized surgeons. 4 years later the new approach fully spread in the community of German hand and neurosurgeons.

Surgeons not only provide new innovative medical practices but also develop new devices (Riskin et al. 2006). A number of historical examples can be found about surgeons that were not only good and successful doctors but also disruptive innovators. For instance, Antonin Jean Desormeaux, a nineteenth-century French surgeon, made significant improvements to an early endoscope, developed by the German surgeon Philipp Bozzini a few decades before. Desormeaux was the first physician to successfully use this device to perform endoscopies. For these reasons, he was known as the "father of endoscopy". A more recent example is the invention made by the American surgeon Thomas Fogarty: a balloon catheter, in 1961. This device allowed surgeons to remove blood clots in a one-hour procedure. After its launch, surgery innovation started to focus on "minimally invasive" technologies that radically simplified several surgical procedures and interventions.

These examples from the past, show how doctors often act as lead users. Indeed, they are able to use their scientific knowledge to anticipate technological trajectories and generate innovations with higher technical relevance that largely impact on corporate innovation in the same technological area (Chatterji and Fabrizio 2008). Lead users, such as surgeons, can develop radical innovations for which established manufacturing firms in the medical equipment industry would not risk or invest (Lettl et al. 2006). Riskin and co-workers (2006) report that a surgeons' personal profile, working context and the daily decision-making activities, train and support this category of physicians in the development of innovative health devices. Surgeons "understand clinical needs and may anticipate future advances and opportunities" (Riskin et al. 2006) and, thus, they often perfectly play the role of lead user.

Recent research found surgeons perform good innovation in some roles but they also risk to hinder it in other situations (Riitta et al. 2017). In particular, professional health users should exploit their knowledge and expertise to develop and practice innovation but should skip, or play a minor role, in the creation and management of new ventures. People with specific managerial profiles and competencies are sometimes, better than doctors in working in key governance roles such as Chief-executive-Officer (CEO).

The evidences about the orientation of public health companies, institutions or single innovators to form online innovation-focused communities are several. A first example is the online platform Doctorpreneurs (www.doctorpreneurs.com). This global community, launched in 2011, connects and provides support and education in entrepreneurship, innovation and new venture creation to medical professionals from all around the world. The members of this community share their common interest of launching their own start-up company. The non-profit organization running and managing the community is based in London. Another similar platform is "Health Innovators" (www.healthinno.org) which is a community of doctors, clinicians, business professionals, programmers, investors, product managers, and more users willing to turn their own innovative health ideas and solutions into reality. The main goal of this community is to find investments for innovative start-up companies created by health professionals. A third case of online community of health user innovators is the Physician Innovation Network (innovationmatch.ama-assn.org) launched by AMA (American Medical Association) in Autumn 2017. This community supports physicians in getting involved in the design cycle of new medical technologies in earlier stages. The platform also establishes a permanent link between doctor-innovators and healthcare companies. Indeed, they can get crucial benefits from physicians, such as qualified feedback on company prototypes and products and services or the access to experts' opinions about specific medical problems through virtual panel discussions.

The German open platform GemeinsamSelten, launched in March 2011, is one of the first cases of virtual communities (used for knowledge creation and development of innovation) reported in healthcare literature (Bullinger et al. 2012). The main goal of the platform was to combine the paradigms of user innovation and open innovation. The platform is made up of 3 main areas: (1) a community area, where participants share general news and information about the platform and its members; (2) a problem area, where people affected by a rare disease can describe their own everyday problems and limitations in terms of quality of life; (3) a solution area, where members develop further initial ideas of other participants and may elaborate new solutions and concepts for health care products and services. Most of the members of the German virtual community are patients, caregivers, interested persons and innovators.[1]

Nurses can also promote innovation and change in healthcare organizations and systems. These particular type of health actors can contribute to the revision of established medical practices, quality improvement of care services, advancement of health policies and health information technologies (Thomas et al. 2016). In particular, Bratton (2017, p. 28) states that: nurses are very creative and good problem-solving employees due to the daily problems they encounter. Whether they are small or big solutions, they not only help patient care be more effective but also indirectly and positively affec their families, other professional staff in the hospitals and the care process in general. Nurses involved in innovative, nursing-directed practice leading to permanent change are named edge runners (American Academy of Nursing 2014). Typical examples of such nurse-driven innovations are new programs to promote breast-feeding in vulnerable infants, new methods to offer assistance to elders that stay at home and programs to improve the skills of caregivers.

These evidences set a clear key difference between doctors and nurses when they innovate. Nurses mostly contribute in the development of soft, process innovation. On the other hand, doctors are also engaged in the innovation of medical practices and care processes, but they also extensively work to develop new or revised medical devices.

2.5   Adoption and Diffusion of User-Generated Healthcare Innovations

As previously mentioned, user-generated innovation also involves innovations done by doctors and nurses. Medicine is a well-known science that requires team work. The integration of multiple health backgrounds in one building and having a common goal makes the medical service multidisciplinary and complete. Along with team work comes interrelationships and influences. As stated by Coleman, et al. in his study: "a doctor will be influenced more by what his colleagues say and do in

---

[1]The results of this research are reported and commented in detail in the next chapter.

Table 2.7 Medical innovations that failed to be widespread

Medical device	Its function	Why it failed to be diffused
Ottawa ankle rules	Highly sensitive bedside diagnostic method for appropriate referral for X-ray.	It has 98% sensitivity, 32% specificity and is highly accepted by patients and health care staff. However, its use in clinical practice remains low.
Computer support systems for treatment of diabetes in primary care	Guideline delineating a standard care of diabetes and a directive supported by evidence.	General practitioners were convinced the evidence was not relevant to their patients in primary care and thought it was only appropriate for acute cases.

Source: WHO (2010)—Barriers to innovation in the field of medical devices

uncertain situations, whenever and wherever they may occur, than in clear-cut situations" (Coleman et al. 2004). This is why hospitals should not be taken as a whole, it is composed by many small units that work together for a main cause. Each unit is not only important but also necessary for the whole machine to work probably. Each unit deserves attention so that the integration of all of them can be done wisely and in an effective manner.

When talking about innovations done by doctors and nurses, all ego and preferences should be put aside as to permit the right evolution of the abovementioned. Interpersonal relationships are important, to have a proper development and diffusion of innovations. When studying the influences and causes of the diffusion of the use of a specific medication amongst doctors, Coleman, et al. concluded that social networks have an impact in how the diffusion is done. First, the influence is greater among colleagues that are connected to others due to professional matters, then it is spread through the friendship network between colleagues, then to the isolated doctors and lastly to all the remaining doctors. Although the diffusion is done through all the doctors in the community, it is done at different times and social networks take a huge role in this. As in any other market, propaganda or diffusion by mouth is key. As human beings, we are social an interdependent and tend to follow habits we see on those that are near us, this is not an exception in the health world. Therefore, when looking at innovations that come either from patients, nurses, doctors or any other health care worker, we should take the time to look at them with attention and evaluate their benefits. When proved to be effective, diffusion of the innovation should be a priority.

In some cases, such diffusion is not reached as expected for many reasons. Examples of some medical innovations that failed to be widespread can be found in Table 2.7.

Medical devices are designed, manufactured and used by a wide range of characters. These can be: the patient, their caregivers, family, friends, acquaintances, students in health-related careers, laboratory technicians, engineers, general practitioners, specialists, nurses, manufacturers, marketers and more. For physicians in specific, innovating does not only involve helping revolutionize the medical world

- Supplier-driven
- Linguistic barriers, i.e. literature not translated into national languages
- Maintenance contracts are missing
- Insufficient staff
- Limited access to technical information or it is unavailable
- Poor maintenance and repair facilities
- Lack of a "training culture", i.e. poor use of a daily protocol and instructions.
- Manuals dense and not easily understandable
- Cost
- No spare parts
- Problems with service maintenance of defective medical devices
- Unrecognized standards for quality control & maintenance
- Inadequate guidelines
- Lack of coordination
- Not enough copies of user manuals for all users
- Procurement issues with mediating ministries (due to acquisition at the central level)
- Direct link broken between producer/vendor & end user
- Shortage of technical expertise
- Lack of funding and trained staff for support
- Weak management culture
- Lack of quality assurance
- Technical information sometimes withheld by industry

Fig. 2.5 Barriers to innovation in medical devices. Source: adaptation (WHO 2010)

and their patients' lives, but it is also a prestigious thing to do. Innovating comes with publications, grants, research and even fame in some cases. Nonetheless, research done by the WHO in 2010 states that the problem is not really the lack of medical devices but the presence of many of them that don't fulfill all the needs the health area needs. Many medical devices have emerged in recent years but have probably not been fully scrutinized, supported or developed to fill in the needs of the market. By not doing so, the medical devices can be lost in time and in hospitals, contributing to dead inventory, loss of opportunity for better equipment to treat patients and even pollution.

Developing countries will sometimes pay the price of these inefficient or out of date medical devices. For instance, in sub-Saharan Africa, for example, almost 70% of equipment is not being actively used. Either due to lack of training on how to use it, lack of support or unclear acquisition processes. More than half of the equipment

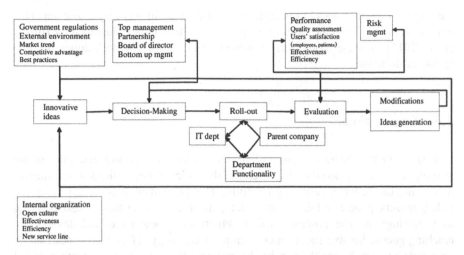

Fig. 2.6 The flow chart of innovative decision-making processes in the healthcare industry. Source: Thakur et al. (2012)

is not properly used or maintained which misses the purpose of the existence of such medical innovations (WHO 2010). Many are the reasons as to why these devices don't get to be used as per intended in developing countries. Figure 2.5 exposes the main barriers to innovation highlighted by the WHO (2010), which might play a role in the lack of diffusion and correct use of medical devices.

The development and commercialization of user-generated innovations in healthcare are common phenomena. These processes are strongly linked with the dynamics of adoption and diffusion promoted by the same innovators. Literature about diffusion and adoption of medical innovation is a rich and established subject. Patterns of diffusion of complex health innovation can greatly differ in terms of rapidness (or slowness) of adoption and prior availability (or lack) of clear evidence about the impact and benefits offered by the new health product or practice (Denis et al. 2002). These variables form a four-quadrant matrix of possible patterns of adoption for complex new health technologies: diffusion success, over-adoption, under-adoption and prudence.

Thakur et al. (2012) developed an interesting inductive framework summarizing the various steps in the decision-making at organizational level for the adoption and diffusion of innovation in healthcare (see Fig. 2.6). The so-called "roll-out" strategy is the core element. This strategy works with systematic procedures based on the collaboration between the IT department of the healthcare organization, the parent company and the department functionality. All the actors must communicate between each other their needs and problems that emerge in the process of development and adoption of the new health technology. The interaction between different departments of the healthcare organization is also crucial.

Various articles provide knowledge and evidence about the specific processes of adoption and diffusion of user-generated health innovations. To these end, the participation of innovators in scientific medical communities is very important. This evidence emerges in all the cases of user-generated techniques illustrated by Hinsch et al. (2014). In these cases, early adopters of novel medical techniques become agents of diffusion.

2.6 Conclusions

Innovation in healthcare is rapidly changing. Several forces and new players are shaping this industry and the value creation dynamics of health firms. User innovation in healthcare has a very long tradition. This phenomenon is crucial for firms, policy-makers, people and the entire society. Its diffusion over time is also evolving as technology is. The process through which these new ideas and devices are reaching people involve social interrelations, technology, IT and even policies. A core type of user in health care is: the patient. They use and consume medical devices, therapies, drugs and health services to preserve their personal quality of life. They often hold a relevant "experiential knowledge" about these products and services which makes them potential user innovators. The next chapter reports the main findings about this rising and fascinating category of user innovators.

Given the fact that the health world involves not only the body but its organs that compose it, making it a very specialized science, many innovations have come to us in order to treat specific ailments. Such list of innovative health products, services and solutions corroborate that healthcare is a very complex industry. A key driver of such complexity is the wide heterogeneity of its industrial and professional players. The heterogeneity of healthcare business segments and the variety of health technologies (drugs, devices, organizational models, procedures and techniques greatly enlarge the number of stakeholders, end-users and intermediate users that can potentially contribute to innovation within this industry.

Either it be X-rays, stethoscopes, sphygmomanometers, ultrasounds, minimally invasive surgeries or prothesis, medical innovations have been present in our lives since many years ago. Human beings by nature, want to excel and become better, some innovations have remained with us since the beginning of time and others have disappeared or been improved. The purpose of this book is, to let the reader inside this not so spoken topic of user innovation and its diffusion. We can sometimes take things in our daily lives for granted because we were either born in the presence of them or have gotten used to having them around. The truth is, we evolve and perfectionate the way we execute tasks and communicate to make our lives more practical. Throughout the next chapters we will further expand on user innovations and the impact they have had or are having in our world.

When deciding to acquire a new technology we tend to fall into "relative advantage" whether we realize it or not. This relative advantage refers to the fact that we are influenced to acquire a certain innovation by judging if the benefits will outweigh the risks of using it. This in turn can either be positive to the diffusion or not of the medical device depending if the vast majority consider it to have more benefits than risks. Relative advantage promotes a technology when the innovation is easier to use than the previous method, often reducing duplicative and inefficient practice (Cain and Mittman 2002). Risk aversion is natural, therefore when a new innovation comes into our lives making sure it is safe and easy to use is key. More attention needs to be put into user innovation and the proper development, marketing and diffusion of it. Medical devices are definitely done to better our lives, to make diagnosing easier, to make treatments more effective and efficient and to simplify the lives of those who have certain pathologies. A proper follow-up can help identify medical devices who are deficient or not holding up to the standard the market needs.

References

AIFA (2017). Report "Criteri per la classificazione dei farmaci innovativi e dei farmaci oncologici innovativi ai sensi dell'articolo 1, comma 402 della legge 11 dicembre 2016, n. 232.". Retrieved from https://www.aifa.gov.it/documents/20142/241044/Allegato_1_1.pdf/66558a13-543c-9643-e67b-85be01547465

Anderson, C. (2007). *The long tail: How endless choice is creating unlimited demand*. London: Random House.

Banta, D. (2003). The development of health technology assessment. *Health Policy, 63*(2), 121–132.

Bodenheimer, T. (2005). High and rising health care costs. Part 2: Technologic innovation. *Annals of Internal Medicine, 142*(11), 932–937.

Boer, H., & Gertsen, F. (2003). From continuous improvement to continuous innovation: A (retro) (per)spective. *International Journal of Technology Management, 26*(8), 805–827.

Bullinger, A. C., Rass, M., Adamczyk, S., Moeslein, K. M., & Sohn, S. (2012). Open innovation in health care: Analysis of an open health platform. *Health Policy, 105*(2), 165–175.

Burns, L. R. (2012). *The business of healthcare innovation*. Cambridge University Press.

Cain, M. & Mittman, R. (2002). Diffusion of innovation in health care. California Health Care Foundation, Institute for the Future.

Chatterji, A. K., & Fabrizio, K. (2008). *The impact of users on technological development: The role of physician innovation in the medical device industry*. Working paper. Fuqua School of Business, Duke University.

Chesbrough, H. (2003). The era of open innovation. *MIT Sloan Management Review, 44*, 35–41.

Coleman, J., Katz, E., & Menzel, H. (2004). The Diffusion of an innovation among physicians. *Sociometry, 20*(4), 253–270.

Consoli, D., & Mina, A. (2009). An evolutionary perspective on health innovation systems. *Journal of Evolutionary Economics, 19*(2), 297.

Dabbs, A. D. V., Myers, B. A., Mc Curry, K. R., Dunbar-Jacob, J., Hawkins, R. P., Begey, A., & Dew, M. A. (2009). User-centered design and interactive health technologies for patients. *Computers, Informatics, Nursing: CIN, 27*(3), 175.

Deichmann, D. & van der Heijde, R. (2016, November). How design thinking turned one hospital into a bright and comfortable place. *Harvard Business Review*.

Deloitte. (2015). *Connected health. How digital technology is transforming health and social care*. Deloitte Centre for Health solutions. Available at: https://www2.deloitte.com/content/dam/Deloitte/pl/Documents/Reports/pl_deloitte-uk-connected-health.pdf

Deloitte (2016). *Top 10 health care innovations: Achieving more for less*. Research report. Retrieved from https://www2.deloitte.com/content/dam/Deloitte/global/Documents/Life-Sciences-Health-Care/gx-lshc-top-10-health-care-innovations-web-friendly.pdf

Deloitte (2018). *2018 Global health care outlook. The evolution of smart health care.* Research report. Retrieved from https://www.hticonference.com/wp-content/uploads/2018/03/gx-lshc-hc-outlook-2018.pdf

Demil, B., & Lecocq, X. (2010). Business model evolution: In search of dynamic consistency. *Long Range Planning, 43,* 227–246.

Denis, J. L., Hébert, Y., Langley, A., Lozeau, D., & Trottier, L. H. (2002). Explaining diffusion patterns for complex health care innovations. *Health Care Management Review, 27*(3), 60–73.

Drummond, M. F., Schwartz, J. S., Jönsson, B., Luce, B. R., Neumann, P. J., Siebert, U., & Sullivan, S. D. (2008). Key principles for the improved conduct of health technology assessments for resource allocation decisions. *International Journal of Technology Assessment in Health Care, 24*(3), 244–258.

Elton, J., & O'Riordan, A. (2016). *Healthcare disrupted: Next generation business models and strategies.* Hoboken, NJ: John Wiley & Sons.

European Network for Health Technology Assessment (EUnetHTA) (2007). *HTA definition.* Internet On line ed. http://www.eunethtanet/HTA/

Eysenbach, G. (2001). What is e-health? *Journal of Medical Internet Research, 3*(2), e20.

Fayssoil, A. (2009). René Laennec (1781–1826) and the invention of the stethoscope. *The American Journal of Cardiology, 104*(5), 743–744.

Fenn, J. (1995). *When to leap on the hype cycle.* Gartner Group, 1.

Gelijns, A., & Rosenberg, N. (1994). The dynamics of technological change in medicine. *Health Affairs, 13*(3), 28–46.

Gilchrist, A. (2016). *Industry 4.0: The industrial internet of things.* Berkeley, CA Apress.

Hajar, R. (2015). History of medicine timeline. *Heart Views: The official journal of the Gulf Heart Association, 16*(1), 43–45.

Hinsch, M. E., Stockstrom, C., & Luthje, C. (2014). User innovation in techniques: A case study analysis in the field of medical devices. *Creativity and Innovation Management, 23*(4), 484–494.

Horbaczewski, A., & Rothaermel, F. (2012). *Merck (in 2009): Open for Innovation?* Brington, MA: Harvard Business School Publishing.

Howitt, P., Darzi, A., Yang, G. Z., Ashrafian, H., Atun, R., Barlow, J., et al. (2012). Technologies for global health. *The Lancet, 380*(9840), 507–535.

Hwang, J., & Christensen, C. M. (2008). Disruptive innovation in health care delivery: A framework for business-model innovation. *Health Affairs, 27*(5), 1329–1335.

Lettl, C., Herstatt, C., & Gemuenden, H. G. (2006). Users' contributions to radical innovation: Evidence from four cases in the field of medical equipment technology. *R&D Management, 36* (3), 251–272.

Mahmud, A., & Parkhurst, M. (2007). *The role of the health care sector in expanding economic opportunity. Corporate social responsibility initiative report, no. 21.* Cambridge, MA: Kennedy School of Government, Harvard University.

McGregor, M., & Brophy, J. M. (2005). End-user involvement in health technology assessment (HTA) development: A way to increase impact. *International Journal of Technology Assessment in Health Care, 21*(2), 263–267.

Medtech Europe (2014). *The European medical technology industry in figures.* Research report. Retrieved from http://www.ub.edu/medicina/grauEB/2014%20The%20European%20medical%20technology%20industry%20in%20figures.pdf

Munos, B. (2009). Lessons from 60 years of pharmaceutical innovation. *Nature Reviews Drug Discovery, 8*(12), 959–968.

Perry, S., & Thamer, M. (1999). Medical innovation and the critical role of health technology assessment. *JAMA, 282*(19), 1869–1872.

Porter, M. E. (2010). What is value in health care? *New England Journal of Medicine, 363*(26), 2477–2481.

Riitta, K., Thatchenkery, S., Christensen, M. Q., & Zenios, S. (2017). Is there a doctor in the house? Expert product users, organizational roles, and innovation. *Academy of Management Journal, 60*(6), 2415–2437.

Riskin, D. J., Longaker, M. T., Gertner, M., & Krummel, T. M. (2006). Innovation in surgery: A historical perspective. *Annals of Surgery, 244*(5), 686–693.

Robinson, T. N., et al. (1998). An evidence-based approach to interactive health communication: A challenge to medicine in the information age. *Journal of American Medical Association., 280*, 1264–1269.

Røtnes, R., & Dybvik Staalesen, P. (2010). *New methods for user driven innovation in the health care sector.* Nordic Council of Ministers, Nordic Innovation Working Paper. Retrieved from http://www.diva-portal.org/smash/get/diva2:707163/FULLTEXT01.pdf

Shaw, B. (1985). The role of the interaction between the user and the manufacturer in medical equipment innovation. *R&D Management, 15*(4), 283–292.

Smits, R. E., & Boon, W. P. (2008). The role of users in innovation in the pharmaceutical industry. *Drug Discovery Today, 13*, 353–359.

Thakur, R., Hsu, S. H., & Fontenot, G. (2012). Innovation in healthcare: Issues and future trends. *Journal of Business Research, 65*(4), 562–569.

Thomas, T. W., Seifert, P. C., & Joyner, J. C. (2016). Registered nurses leading innovative changes. *OJIN: The Online Journal of Issues in Nursing, 21*(3).

Timmermans, S., & Berg, M. (2003). The practice of medical technology. *Sociology of Health & Illness, 25*(3), 97–114.

Topol, E. J., & Hill, D. (2012). *The creative destruction of medicine: How the digital revolution will create better health care.* New York: Basic Books.

Tran, V. T., & Ravaud, P. (2016). Frugal innovation in medicine for low resource settings. *BMC Medicine, 14*(1), 102.

Wager, K. A., Lee, F. W., & Glaser, J. P. (2017). *Health care information systems: A practical approach for health care management.* San Francisco, CA: John Wiley & Sons.

World Health Organization. (2010). *A stepwise approach to identify gaps in medical devices* (availability matrix and survey methodology): Background paper 1, August 2010 (No. WHO/HSS/EHT/DIM/10.1). Geneva: World Health Organization.

WHO (2020). *World Health Organization.* Retrieved from https://www.who.int/health-technology-assessment/about/healthtechnology/en/

Xia, F., Yang, L. T., Wang, L., & Vinel, A. (2012). Internet of things. *International Journal of Communication Systems, 25*(9), 1101.

Zeschky, M., Widenmayer, B., & Gassmann, O. (2011). Frugal innovation in emerging markets. *Research-Technology Management, 54*(4), 38–45.

Chapter 3
Patient Innovation

Abstract In this chapter we fully discuss patient innovation and patient engagement. Patient Innovation is when "patients or their nonprofessional caregivers (e.g., parents, family members, spouses or partners) modify or develop a treatment, behavioural strategy, technical aid or a medical device to cope with their ailment" (Habicht et al., Die Unternehmung 66(3):277–294, 2012). Patient innovation is a relatively new concept that has caught the attention of researchers in the recent years specially on developed countries. It's through patient engagement that health actors can help make their innovations a success. This is done by first acknowledging their innovation, getting involved and promoting it. Patient engagement can be explained as "how much information flows between a patient and a provider, how active a role the patient has in care decisions, and how involved the patient or patient organization are in health organization decisions and in policy making". Later on, in the chapter, a more detailed explanation of patient engagement can be found.

Keywords Patient innovation · Patient engagement · Service co-creation

3.1 Introduction

Few things can make us connect to others like testimonies of life do. Mary Temple Grandin, born in Massachusetts in 1947 was diagnosed with "brain damage" at age 2 and was recommended to be institutionalized. Her mother was forthrightly against it and decided to take her to therapies and stimulation programs that permitted her to interact better with others. During high school she met her science teacher, William Carlock who changed her life. After visiting her uncles' farm and looking at how cows calmed downed after being squeezed with two metal flaps, together with Carlock she created the Hug Box or "squeeze machine" to get the same effect on herself (Squeeze machine 2019). People living with autism disorders find it difficult

Chapter written by Francesco Schiavone and Cristina M. Thiebaud. The authors thank Pasqualina Malafronte for the bibliometric analysis reported in the chapter.

F. Schiavone, *User Innovation in Healthcare*, SpringerBriefs in Health Care Management and Economics, https://doi.org/10.1007/978-3-030-44256-9_3

to have social interactions and are sensible to sensory stimulations making it difficult to turn to humans for comfort. During her college years, her peers criticized and made fun of her box, this prompted. Carlock to suggest her to evaluate the efficacy of the device through experiments. The squeeze machine is now sold by the Therafin Corporation in cooperation with her, to autistic patients (Temple Grandin 1992).

Patient Innovation is when "patients or their nonprofessional caregivers (e.g., parents, family members, spouses or partners) modify or develop a treatment, behavioural strategy, technical aid or a medical device to cope with their ailment" (Habicht et al. 2012). Many definitions are currently being used to define patient innovation, it is a new interest in healthcare management and therefore research around it is still being done. Developed countries are mostly interested in this new influence and the impact it has on the health care system. Throughout this chapter we discuss two important terms related to patients and their role in health care; these are: Patient Engagement and Patient Innovation.

Patient engagement as explained by Carman Kristin et al. is defined as "how much information flows between patients and providers, how active the role the patient has in care decisions, and how involved the patient or patient organization becomes in health organization decisions and in policy making" (Carman et al. 2013). Although it is a two-end communication system there is always one part that has more power and influence than the other. For many years, health professionals have had the power over patients by deciding their care pathway without having their input. It's not until recent years that the shift has gone to patients and their needs, now both the health care providers and patients have a decision-making authority and together work as a team to find the pathway that best suits each individual case. The power, accountability and responsibility are now being shared, making the flow of information bidirectional and empowering patients.

3.2   Patient Engagement

Having control of one's body, mental and physical health, emotions and surroundings can be challenging if not presented with the right tools to properly manage them. Through Patient engagement, patients take their health into their hands by having a more active role. "Engaged patients have a better ability to make informed decisions about their care options. This in addition helps in the correct use of resources when aligned with a patients' priorities. Making it more sustainable in health systems worldwide" (Patient Engagement: Technical Series on Safer Primary Care 2016). A doctor-patient relationship is a two-way communication system that makes the medical doctor the author and the patient the co-author of their health status. While medical doctors may be more focused on the diagnosis, treatment, financial and logistics aspects, the patient will usually be more concerned on their health and safety. This two-way communication gives both characters a mutual accountability. Taking into account the patients' priorities doubts and concerns makes the care more straightforward, effective and holistic.

In order to have an effective patient engagement, patients and their families, carers and health care providers have to be involved. While taking into consideration all these extra characters, the active involvement and the support is greater. At an organizational level, patients and families can be engaged in the design or development of patient-centred processes and systems, for example as members of advisory committees (Frampton and Patrick 2008). Human beings are social and emotional creatures by nature, feeling connected to others in a safe and integral way helps create confidence and courage to carry one's life in a better way. It's only through communication, education and constant actualization that patient engagement can be successful and beneficial to both the patient and the organization.

3.2.1   PROMS and PREMS

In order to be engaged, patients must feel supported, satisfied with the services they are being provided, listened and comprehended. When patients and organizations are in tune, things flow easier and more effectively. Collecting information about the patient experience and outcomes of care may be the starting point for engaging patients (Patient Engagement: Technical Series on Safer Primary Care 2016). Through the collection of these types of information a better insight of their needs, values and preferences can be gathered. It can be done through surveys, interviews, questionnaires, focal group discussions and online feedback. Indicators and widely used patient reported measures can also aid in searching weak points in the system. New ways of capturing this information are always being researched. Two widely used and effective questionnaires used worldwide are the Patient-reported outcome measures (PROMs) and the Patient-reported experience measures (PREMs). Although they are both usually used for research, their use in everyday service centres can be helpful, as it is a direct reflection of how patients perceive their own health and the quality of service they are receiving.

The Patient-reported outcome measures (PROMs) are questionnaires that measure the patients' view of their health status, disease and the treatment they received. It gathers information and measures aspects of health-like symptoms, symptom burdens, overall quality of life, distress and functionality ability. PROMs can be used to evaluate a specific condition or in a general way. It can be used by healthcare providers to monitor how the patient feels after being diagnosed and about the treatment they received. They can also be used by health care institutions to improve patient centered quality services. All human bodies work different so even if patients have the same diagnoses their health statuses can vary, the way they perceive it, how they function daily, how they cope with an ailment and the limitations they have. Therefore satisfaction can vary depending of the eye of the beholder.

Measuring the effect, a treatment has on a patient's daily life, is subjective as we can't rely on scientific and clinical exams for this. The PROMS aim to measure: Health-related quality of life, patient satisfaction, Physical functioning, psychological state, signs and symptoms, social functioning, treatment adherence and utility or usefulness (Patient-reported outcomes (PROs) assessment 2019). Through the recollection of all previously mentioned, an integrative view of the patients' life can be gathered.

The Patient-reported experience measures (PREMs) are questionnaires that measure the patients' perceptions and satisfaction of their experience with an organization whilst receiving care (Patient-Reported Experience Measures 2015). Not only is it an insight of their preferences and needs but also a direct reflection of the service, the provider and the institution's quality of service. The overall experience a patient receives while visiting a health care institution has an impact on the way they decide to take an active role. Prolonged waiting time, poor quality of communication, no support, lack of comprehension of the care they are being given and confusion in the pathways taken during medical care can cause adherence to treatment to fail. PREMs are often used in the wider population and in non-specific settings such an outpatient department. The information they provide through feedback helps detect the problems that can be affecting the quality of services provided. It is not a way to see if proper treatment is being given, but a way to test how services are being provided to patients.

Nothing works better and cheaper than word-of-mouth propaganda which directly reflects the probability of recommending the service to friends, colleagues and family. Happy and satisfied patients are more likely to adhere to treatments and to come back for follow ups.

Although PROMS and PREMS are usually easy to implement they can have some limitations with people with low literacy or people with learning disabilities. People are usually ashamed of accepting their low literacy and others are not conscient of the literacy level they have, which might provide incomplete information. Helping them fill out the questionnaire might also cause them not to be completely honest due to the fear of being judged or mistreated for being honest. Inaccurate completion of PROMs might fail to include these subpopulations and alienate them and their perspectives and needs from healthcare practices. A good approach for this reality would be to do a PROM/PREM easy to understand and answer and also giving them the option to complete it at home with the help of one of their family members.

There is no exact way of developing a PROM/PREM questionnaire and although there are guidelines available on how to make them, making them perfect is not only hard to achieve but also subjective. However, many have been developed worldwide that are personalized to each hospital and country's realities. When making these kinds of questionnaires, the goal is to make it easy to comprehend and answer. To name a few available worldwide: Consumer Assessment of Healthcare Providers and Systems (CAHPS), Quality from the Patients' Perspective (QPP) and QPP—Shortened (QPPS), Picker Patient Experience Questionnaire (PPE-15), NHS Inpatient Survey (NHSIS), Scottish Inpatient Patient Experience Survey (SIPES), Hong Kong Inpatient Experience Questionnaire (HKIEQ), Patient Experience Questionnaire (PEQ), Norwegian Patient Experience Questionnaire (NORPEQ), In-Patient Experiences of Health Care (I-PAHC), Patient Perceptions of Care (PPQ), *Hospital Consumer Assessment of Healthcare Providers and Systems (HCAHPS)* used in

USA, Patient Health Engagement Scale (PHE-S), EuroQol EQ-5D, Patient-Reported Outcomes Measurement Information System (PROMIS) and more (Weldring and Smith 2013).

3.2.2 Patient Engagement and Integral Care

Patient engagement and the way they take an active role on their health, as co-authors of it, is crucial to the success of their treatments and involvement with the health care sector. Clear communication between the patient and the healthcare provider is important, information needs to be handed to patients in a simple and comprehensible way. The process of communication starts by providing a comfortable and amicable environment for this interaction to occur. It is followed by a clear outflow of information, an active listening and constant positive feedback. Improving communication and educating both patients and health care providers to view health care as a partnership between the patient and the provider is important (Patient Engagement: Technical Series on Safer Primary Care 2016). Once both parties are on the same page a plan can be formulated that takes into account the patients' preferences, concerns, doubts and interest. This is when goals are set and empowerment or activation is first encountered. Together a pathway can be built making decision-making easier and uncomplicated while taking into consideration both the medical doctor's knowledge and the patients' needs. It is important to have harmony and fluidity when having a mutual agreement which permits transparent communication. All of what is being shared between the two parties should also be properly documented (Wheat et al. 2018). The end result is a quality continuity of care and successful follow-ups with honest and helpful feedback.

To have an integral health care it is important to focus on quality of service, effectiveness, timeliness and patient centered services. As the world we are currently living in is evolving at a faster pace, technology is a crucial and important part of healthcare. The availability of information online makes it easier for patients to access it and get informed. Patients are not only concerned with the diagnosis they will get but also with the way health care services are being provided to them. There is an increased interested by them to get transparent, equitable, efficient, personalized and fair services. Although health care providers are expected to work on primary prevention with patients, sometimes it's the patients themselves that initiate these conversations. Health care providers should be up-to-date on current health trends and use it to their advantage to get better adherence to treatments and to educate patients on well-known diseases and their effects on health. Social media, videos, leaflets, brochures, telephone calls, text messages and online surveys should be used to educate and reach out to patients. An educated and informed patient is more likely to seek for help when they detect anomalies and are also more likely to share positive experiences.

Patient engagement is as a strategy that tries to target the "triple aim" by improving outcomes, providing better care or patient experience and reducing per capita costs (Amann et al. 2016). As the current industrialized world continues to expand, more and more chronic diseases are beginning to be a burden. During the last decades, the world has experienced a demographic and epidemiological transition characterized by an aging population and an increase in chronic health conditions (Kaplan et al. 2017). The proper management and plan of care of chronic diseases is not only important but also necessary. Hypertension, being a prevalent chronic condition is a great candidate for making patients have an active role on their disease management. Uncontrolled hypertension can cause organ failures such as in the heart, brain, kidneys and eyes and can also leave patients with long-term adverse effects. A proper log-in of a patient's blood pressure (BP) can help them realize how they are doing and what changes should be made if their blood pressure is not controlled. Studies have proven that involving patients in their own health care makes them more active and efficient in the management and treatment of their disease. Self-measuring of the blood pressure connects the patient to their reality and to their health care provider. Being aware of what their blood pressure values are on a day to day basis helps them makes better decisions on managing their health status. These decisions are linked to physical activity, diet, stress and medication adherence (Mc Namara et al. 2014). Both the BP monitoring done by health professionals and by the self-monitoring are important to confirm results. When done in a team not only is it more effective but makes patients feel closer to their health care providers. This makes it easier for health care providers to provide educational interventions, advices and assessment of lifestyle risks. The consequences of non-engagement may include preventable illness and suffering, suboptimal health outcomes, increases in health disparities, and wasted resources (Barello et al. 2012).

3.3 Patient Innovation

Patient innovators are "patients or their nonprofessional caregivers (e.g., parents, family members, spouses or partners) who modify or develop a treatment, behavioural strategy, technical aid or a medical device to cope with their ailment" (Habicht et al. 2012). This interest in developing new devices, treatments or aids is due to the lack of them in the market or the difficulty of personalizing existing methods. The interest and need of new solutions, devices, techniques or treatments enriches current researches being conducted. Patient innovators are often crucial actors for the development of innovations improving the quality of life of people affected by rare diseases (Oliveira et al. 2015). At the same time, it makes the patient and its surrounding social circle more involved with a proper and more personalized health care. This approach helps transform the conventional disease-centered care to a more patient-centered care where they take actions into their hands.

In 1960 a "ladder of citizen participation" was published that focuses on the effects of citizen involvement in planning processes in the United States. The ladder is composed of three levels and each level has its subdivisions; it shows the participation that ranges from low to high (Arnstein 2007). The bottom level corresponds to the "non-participation" group and its sub-levels: Manipulation and Therapy. The purpose of people who work with people who fall in this category is to educate them. The middle level is "Degrees of tokenism" and is composed of three sub-levels: Informing, consultation and placation. People who fall in this category are small groups of people that represent minorities or underrepresented groups. However, they lack power and fall in risk of not having follow-ups after they give their insights. The higher level corresponds to "Degrees of citizen power" and its sub-levels: Partnership, Delegated Power and Citizen Control. When referring to partnership, this involves the public and the service providers and the way retro alimentation helps improve and negotiate better services. The higher the level the more the citizen power and the less they can relate and feel connected to the ones in lower levels. Although the ladder was not specifically made for the health care it is applicable, nowadays patient involvement can be classified in the first two levels: Non-Participation and Tokenism.

Traditionally, health professionals have been in charge of research and devices and treatment development with a more paternalistic approach. A new shift is now present in which the public is now taking an important role in development and use of new concepts and solutions in health care (Bullinger-Hoffmann et al. 2012). The incorporation of the public's view, suggestions and recommendations enriches what is being done and opens the possibility of integrating their needs and preferences to mainstream devices and treatments currently used. Through the conjoint approach of patients, their health providers and organizations a more holistic service can be provided. By doing so, satisfaction increases as well as quality of services, interrelationships and even costs.

Many discoveries have been done throughout time, some were intentional and others were coincidence or the result of multiple errors. Whatever the reason for a discovery is, it is undeniable that the impact discoveries have on our lives are huge either for the good or the bad. In the healthcare system, on-going research has and will always be present, there is a constant interest to find better, cheaper and more efficient ways of doing things. Although medicine and medical treatments and instruments have been present since the beginning of mankind, it's not until the mid-1700s that we have proof and registry of the first medical devices being used.

A letter written by the Duke of Milan to his ambassador in Florence ordering three dozen eyeglasses including "a dozen that are suitable for near vision" (for the elderly), proves the existences of eyeglasses in this age (Rachel Kilgas 2018). Around the same time Benjamin Franklin invented the flexible catheter for his brother John, who suffered from bladder stones. Almost 65 years later Rene Laennec, a French physician invented the stethoscope. In the 1840s Dr. Crawford W. Long performed his first operation using diethyl ether as an anesthetic. He pressed an ether-soaked towel against the patient's face to put him to sleep and then removed one of the two tumors from his neck. Discoveries like: The X-ray, electrocardiograms, laparoscopes, electroencephalograms, pacemakers, dialysis, kidney transplant, portable defibrillators, CT scanner, HIV medications and many more have revolutionized medicine. Not only have they helped innovate health care but also made it easier and more effective to diagnose and treat diseases.

Healthcare has been assigning the authority and responsibility of health care services, the implementation of new diagnostic tools and the creation of new treatments to health professionals only. "Nowadays, the patient's voice is taken into consideration because it seems to have a great contribution in obtaining better health outcomes. This in turn enhances a patient's care and cure experience and improves illness self-management and adherence to therapies. It also helps decrease care costs (Barello et al. 2012)". Patients are the nucleus of health care; they are also the solution to many of the problems if time is taken to hear their ideas and concerns. Changing the current status quo can be challenging however not impossible. Patients are now more interested in safety measures when receiving healthcare services and the consequences of not having them. Taking into account their needs to make more innovative and personalized devices, treatments and services benefits all parties involved.

Henry William Chesbrough an American professor born in 1956, specialized as an organizational theorist with a bachelor's in economics, an MBA and a PhD coined the term open innovation. His book on Open Innovation talks about the importance of the transition from a Closed Innovation in which a company has complete control of the development of a product until it is released to the market to a more Open Innovation System. The open innovation approach as stated by him "means that great ideas can come from inside but also from outside of the company. This approach makes external ideas and external paths in the market as important as internal ideas". This is a contrast to the Closed Innovation era (Chesbrough 2003). The purpose of this integrative approach is to find the missing pieces provided by external views to make services or products better. These external views can be given by suppliers, the competition and most importantly, the patients.

Let's take the example of the Dana-Farber Cancer Institute. In this institution they decided to take into account patients and their family members and made them part of the decision-making process. They played an important role in helping succeed in quality improvement and were part of the hiring decisions as well as in developing and providing staff training (Carman et al. 2013). This kind of impact on an organization has direct influence on the institution itself but also on current and future patients. When it comes to policies and government approaches, the patient's insight is also beneficial. Not only does it allow an unbiased approach but it also takes into consideration the patient's perspectives. When they are involved in government health plans, patients will better reflect the community's concerns and the target can be better identified by government leaders. Open innovation allows the combination of ideas given by employees inside an organization and people outside an organization. As stated by Chesbrough:

> If the smart people within your company are aware of, connected to, and informed by the efforts of smart people outside, then your innovation process will reinvent fewer wheels. What's more, your internal efforts will be multiplied many times through their embrace of others' ideas and inspiration (Chesbrough, Henry W, 2003).

3.3.1   Lorenzo Odone

Lorenzo Odone, born in 1978, was an Italian-American boy suffering of adrenoleu-kodystrophy (ALD) from the age of 6. People with this disease gradually become mute, deaf, blind and paralysed. Death usually arrives within 2 years after the diagnosis. Lorenzo's parents, Augusto and Michaela actively reacted to this situation and together with a British chemist invented a special treatment, the so-called Lorenzo Oil to contrast the illness of their son (Lorenzo's Oil. The Myelin Project 2018). Thanks to this self-made treatment, that halts the progression of ALD by normalizing the accumulation of the very long chain fatty acids in the brain, Lorenzo survived until 2008, when he died at the age of 30. The story of Augusto, Michaela, and Lorenzo Odone inspired the famous movie entitled Lorenzo's oil (starring Nick Nolte and Susan Sarandon). Both Augusto and Michaela Odone are the founders of The Myelin Project that now distributes the oil internationally.

Sometimes necessity, other times rare undiagnosed diseases with unknown treatments and other times misheard patients can lead to life changing innovations. Adding patients to the equation and their contributions and ideas helps Research and Development be more fluent and faster. There is growing evidence that the future health care can rely upon strong involvement of patients (Zejnilovic et al. 2016). This involvement can be profited by their ideas, their capacities, new approaches of treatments and their outsider views.

3.3.2   Runway of Dreams Foundation

When Oliver came home from school and asked his mom if he could wear jeans as his friends did, she was faced with a challenge. Oliver was diagnosed as a baby with muscular dystrophy that causes loss of muscular strength. His mom, Mindy Scheier had a background in fashion and designed jeans that fit over his leg braces and that would be easy to manipulate by Oliver (My Runway of Dreams Story by Mindy Scheier 2015), for her it was important that her son could feel independent. This incident made her realize that adaptive clothing has a great impact on people with disabilities, making them feel confident while also being trendy. She created Runway of Dreams Foundation in 2016 and has even made a collaboration with Tommy Hilfiger. She is now dedicated to bringing accessible and fashionable adaptive clothing to the millions of people who live with disabilities around the world (Mindy Scheier, Blue Ocean-shift-strategy-leadership 2004–2019). Not only did she help her son feel included and self-confident, she is now changing other children's lives by helping them feel part of society. Her goal is to work with as many mainstream brands as possible (Mindy Schieir 2016). Although her contribution to health is not a medical device, a treatment option or a technological advancement, it is helping children with disability feel included. Confidence, attention to mental health and feeling part of a community helps patients feel empowered and more prone to sharing their experiences with health providers. When patients feel part of a system, communication is better, which in turn helps to propiciate a healthier and better interconnected health system.

3.3.3 Patient Innovation Drive

To overcome difficulties imposed by their health disorder, or the disease of people close to them, patients and caregivers often have to innovate (Zejnilovic et al. 2016). Although innovations made by patients are mostly appreciated by their community and health care providers in direct contact with them, most of the time they go unnoticed to the rest of the world. Evidence showed by surveys shows that the dispersion of user innovations is actually low. This was concluded after implementing general population surveys. The diffusion of innovations varied from 5% to 17%, being peer-to-peer exchanges the most common diffusion pathway (Fursov et al. 2017). This low diffusion can cause unnecessary duplication efforts to occur, causing a market failure and a misuse of resources. A cooperation among health givers, patients and caregivers is essential in the success of diffusion of patient innovations. Using their skills and complementing them with those of the people that surround them, not only helps lower costs but makes all feel part of the process and the change. Feeling supported in turn, incentivizes patients to share their innovations.

Patient innovation activity and the activity of health care professionals are complementary rather than competing activities (Zejnilovic et al. 2016). Patients trust the medical doctors, nurses and health professionals they are in contact with on health-related information they provide them with. Nurses are often portrayed by patients as the health providers who most make them feel as full engaged partners in the process of care quality (Barello et al. 2012). This is important to know, so that improvements and future plans and system changes are centred on the way nurses approach patients. Assuring a comfortable, open and caring relationship between nurses, health providers and patients helps maximize the care and the probabilities of patients sharing their ideas. This relationship should be used as a bridge to develop health innovations.

Health professionals' way of thinking needs to be changed in order to be successful with the propagation of patient innovation. To create a more supportive environment, it is necessary to raise awareness of patient innovations from the early days at medical, nursing, and other health care professional schools (Zejnilovic et al. 2016). This approach is not only cost efficient but also revolutionizes how medicine has been done for years. As the world evolves, more information is available and easier ways to do things surge up. Patients need to be empowered and organized in order for them to feel part of the innovation process. Listening to them and their ideas is key to changing the current health model into a more patient centred one.

Some innovations may not seem as impactful as others; however, an innovation is intended to make patients' life easier and make them feel included in society. One simple example of innovation made by patients in conjunction with their community is the use of tattoos to cover up scars. A study done in January 2008 by G.A. Spyropoulou et al., shows three cases of patients that decided to seek help with local tattooers to cover up surgical scars. The tattoos covered abdominoplasty scars and also replicated a breast areola in another case (Spyropoulou and Fatah 2008). Tattoos are widely known to be used on patients with post breast mastectomy and posterior breast implants to simulate an areola. Other patients are deciding to tattoo on their bodies the medicines they are allergic to, their religions, Do Not Resucitate (DNR) claims, diagnosis, medical treatments and more. When patients take into their own hands to find solutions, interesting and innovative ways come out. It is important to make them feel part of the health care system so these ideas are properly shared with the rest of the world.

3.3.4   The Shower Shirt

Lisa F. Crites, an American breast cancer survivor invented the Shower Shirt with the help of her family. This is the first and only patented, water-resistant garment to protect chest surgery patients while showering (Lisa F. Crites, The shower Shirt Company). After having a double mastectomy surgery in 2009 she was forced to take a shower using trash bags to protect her drain sites. Finding it uncomfortable to wear trash bags she decided to design a shirt with her brother who is an architect and did the computerized design for her. She then created a prototype with the help of her aunt and cousins and after five prototypes she finally got it right. It is considered a Class 1 Medical device by the Food and Drug Administration (FDA) in United States. Each medical device is classified by them depending on the risks for the user associated with the device (Regulatory Controls for Medical Devices 2018). A Class 1 Medical Device is considered to have a low to moderate risk when used by a patient and/or user (What's the Difference Between the FDA Medical Device Classes? 2018). Not only has Lisa been awarded as an innovator but is also now the distributor of the Shower Shirt which is being sold world-wide. Not only have post mastectomy patients been benefited by her innovation but also patients with chest surgeries that include hemodialysis, cardiac, lung, hernia, rotator cuff, neuro-stimulation, and external defibrillator patients. She wanted to make a difference and is now allowing other patients to take showers in a safe and comfortable way.

3.3.5   Patient Innovation Process

Patient Innovation is also known as: patient-driven innovation, patient-led innovation, patient-driven healthcare, people-powered health, participatory healthcare, user-centered healthcare, open source healthcare, and data-driven healthcare (Maffei et al. 2019). Patients can become innovators when they come up with an idea that covers their needs related to a disease or to make their quality of life better. Health providers should encourage this brainstorming of ideas when approached by a patient or a caregiver because together they can come up with better ideas. Patient innovation is a new wave emerging in the healthcare systems, especially in developed countries. Although it is a new branch it has sparked interest in many, especially in the economics area, healthcare management and those in charge of social innovation.

Recently, a group of researchers in Milano came up with a system called the *MakeToCareLadder* which can be used to synthetize and visualize in an orderly manner, the process through which an idea, can be developed and finalized as a product and available to the public. They divided the ladder in four phases (Maffei et al. 2019): The Design and Prototype Phase (A), Business Development Phase (B), Regulatory Verification Phase (C) and the Distribution and Supply Phase (D). Phase A corresponds to the first step of the process in which the idea is developed either by the person that needs it or by an observer that detects the need and where a prototype is done. Phase B corresponds to the production of a unique product (tailor-made or personalized), limited series and mass production. Phase C corresponds to device classification, declaration of conformity, pre-marketing clinical investigation and assessment and lastly manufacturer and device registration. This phase is when a clinical point of view is considered, nevertheless it is not mandatory for all innovations, for example apps and software do not require it. However, innovations like medical devices do need to be approved or need to have the CE legal mark in Europe for example, to be able to enter the market (CE marking approval for medical devices in Europe 2019). Lastly Phase D is composed by: medical visit and prescription, authorization and supply, testing and post-market investigation.

It is important to acknowledge patients and caregivers who reach out to healthcare providers to express their concerns, ideas and suggestions. It is only through great communication and teamwork efforts that these projects can be developed and benefit as many as possible. Whether it is through a product or a service, these innovations can help reduce research investment, time and efforts. Not all innovations are directed to treatment, some are focused on facilitating daily activities and others to better the quality of life. Regardless of the approach an innovation can have, it is important to take them all into consideration. It's the user's feedback and retro alimentation that helps make services and products better. Their point of view is different to that of product and services providers. Patient innovation permits the healthcare system to be enriched by having an insight voice as well as making doctor-patient relationships stronger. It is a win-win situation and makes the innovation process smoother and more efficient.

3.4 Bibliometric Analysis

The growing application of bibliometric research in social sciences describes and maps complex phenomena causing fragmentation of academic research to increase. Indeed, this research methodology helps to build a unitary view of the various elements of knowledge about certain phenomena. This section reports the results of a bibliometric analysis about the concept of patient innovation. The purpose of bibliometric analysis is to describe research and represent science through maps and graphs. This is also called science mapping. Such method does not only allow to present and summarise literature review, it also allows to highlight the relationships between topics and authors. Bibliometric analysis provides a synthesis of the main references for a specific disciplinary field or a specific theme. This type of analysis, with the support of maps and other graphic visualizations, applies mathematical and statistical methods to find documents and publication models about a specific topic.

To this end, the open-source software Bibliometrix was used. The software is freely distributed via the websites www.bibliometrix.org and www.bibliometrix.com. The analysis was organised in the following steps: (1) identification of the key themes; (2) research design; (3) data collection: (4) data analysis; (5) data visualization; and (6) data interpretation with descriptive statistics, data reduction techniques or mappings. The database used for this research is Web of Science by Thomson Reuters, which is the main scientific database for economic and business journals. The author set the search procedure to find, within articles published in academic management journals (in English), the following keywords: patient innovation, innovation by patient, caregiver innovation. The keywords are linked by the logical operator OR.

A sample of 297 articles was extracted from various online scientific databases. Figures 3.1 and 3.2 reports the most cited papers and most productive countries about patient innovation. Twenty papers stand out amongst those that cite "patient innovation" in the above graph. The top one is that of Brown T, 2008 in the Harvard Business Review journal with more than 800 citations. Followed by that of Edmondson AC, 2001 in the Administrative Science Quarterly with over 700 citations. Just under is Botteman MF, 2003 in the Pharmacoeconomics journal with more than 500 citations. Also, in the top 5 we find Eisenmann T, 2006 in the Harvard Business Review journal and Kaplan RS, 2001 also in the Harvard Business Review with almost 400 and more than 350 citations respectively. As can be seen, the Harvard Business Review journal is predominant in the top 5 most cited documents. Out of the 20 documents highlighted they take part in 7 of them. The Pharmacoeconomics' journal follows with 3 mentions, Value Health with 2 and all others with 1.

The most productive top countries concerning author's country were USA, United Kingdom, Italy, Netherlands and Canada. Out of the top five countries, America is predominant followed by Europe and the countries with less publications are New Zealand, Ireland and Russia.

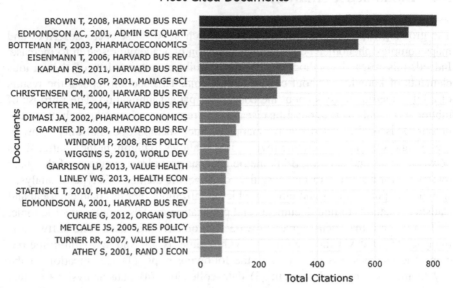

Fig. 3.1 Most cited papers about patient innovation (Source: Our elaboration)

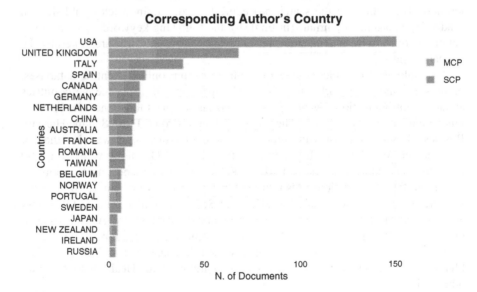

Fig. 3.2 Most productive countries on corresponding author's country (Source: Our elaboration)

As reported in Table 3.1, the scientific journals that published more articles on the subject of interest are: Value in Health (77 articles), Pharmacoeconomics (46), Journal of Nursing Management (34), European Journal of Health Economics (17), Health Economics (14) and Harvard Business Review (13). All previous

Table 3.1 The magazines with more articles on the subject of interest

Sources	Articles
Value in Health	77
Pharmacoeconomics	46
Journal of Nursing Management	34
European Journal of Health Economics	17
Health Economics	14
Harvard Business Review	13
Journal of Health Economics	9
Research Policy	9
Applied Health Economics and Health Policy	8
Health Economics Review	6
Business Process Management Journal	4
European Journal of Operational Research	4
Interfaces	4
Journal of Public Economics	4
Journal of Service Management	4
Management Science	4
Service Industries Journal	4
Total Quality Management & Business Excellence	4
Human Relations	3
IFKAD 2017:12th International Forum on Knowledge Asset Dynamics: Knowledge Management in the 21st Century: Resilience Creativity and Co-creation	3

Source: Our elaboration

mentioned are the top 6 out of 20 mentioned in the table. From which half correspond to an economics background magazine, as reported in Table 3.2, in which the most used key-words in the analysed articles are listed.

According to author keywords the most used keywords in the articles were: Innovation (54 articles), Care (43), Health-care (29), Management (27) and Performance (22).

Figure 3.3 identifies the relationships between the keywords and, therefore, between the specific topics covered in the articles.

The *co-word* analysis has identified the *conceptual structure* of the research. This analysis is based on *multiple correspondence analysis (MCA)*. The software used independently divides the articles into more *"clusters"*, based on the variables identified by the same as relevant. As can be seen from the graph in Fig. 3.3, *bibliometrix* has identified X cluster of analysis. Depending on whether they are positioned farther to the right or to the left, they more or less approach the variables identified by the software as relevant. For example, the keywords *"accounting restatement"* and *"internal control"* are in the same cluster (the extreme one on the right), as well as *"asymmetric"* and *"investor"* in another (bottom left); *"Strategy"* and *"shareholders wealth"*, instead, are found together in the cluster at the center. Compared to these clusters, the position they take between them is interesting. For example, while the aforementioned seconds are closer, and therefore have

Words	Occurrences
Innovation	54
Care	43
Health-care	29
Management	27
Performance	22
Cost-effectiveness	21
Impact	21
Systems	19
Health	18
Model	17
Hospitals	15
Organizations	15
Quality	15
Technology	15
Outcomes	14
United-States	14
Work	14
Knowledge	13
Information	12
Quality-of-life	12

Table 3.2 The most used keywords in the articles on the subject of interest

Source: Our elaboration

some connection, the first is more detached. It can be deduced, therefore, that it contains research topics that are still relevant, but that are less associated with other research topics by scholars.

3.5 Patient Innovation on Social Media

The phenomenon of Patient Innovation (PI) also received attention on social media. Over the last few years, at least three online communities emerged to link patients, caregivers, doctors, researchers and other practitioners together. We briefly review them in the present subsection. These health-related online websites are platforms made to share and explore a specific disease, health device or to share personal experiences. These kinds of platforms allow patients to exchange information, doubts, fears, triumphs and find support.

Not only are they beneficial to the patients but also to the firms that are interested in patient feedback. Three types of virtual communities have been distinguished: firm-hosted, firm-related, and independent online communities (Amann et al. 2016). Firm-hosted communities are initiated, maintained, and governed by commercial producers. The second type, firm-related communities, are initiated and governed by community members in a self-organized process. Lastly, independent communities

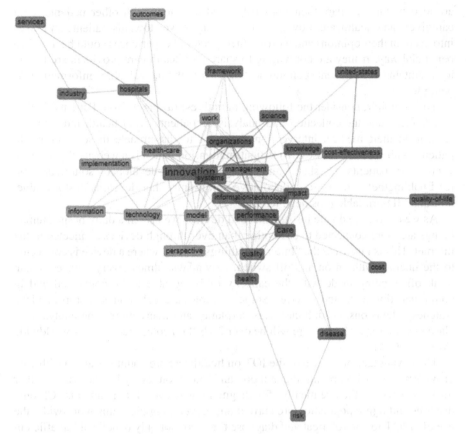

Fig. 3.3 Mapping of the keywords used by the articles on the subject of interest, with the "co-occurrences" technique (Source: Our elaboration)

have no link to professional or commercial organizations and are driven solely by the community members and their epistemic goals.

Online health platforms can be used by firms to capture innovative ideas provided by patients since it's usually the place they go to share and inform their concerns and ideas to make health care services better. Having multiple inputs and collaborations by outsiders in the platforms makes a competition emerge that benefits not only patients but also the firms. This is so, because, competition helps make ideas better, efficient and easier to execute. These online communities are usually managed and dominated by a small, active core community of self-selected individuals (Amann et al. 2016). It's important to note that this self-selection is advantageous because people who are usually active, do research and are interested in helping available resources better for theirs and others benefit.

The ongoing feedback and interaction made by patients should be an incentive for firms to have a more active role and have better communication with end users. Most patients are willing to share their personal health information for research and are also willing to share their knowledge and solutions with other patients, their caregivers and healthcare providers. If the focus moves towards patients and takes into account their opinions and worries, their personal experiences could be used in a beneficial way. If they are not willing to share and health care providers are failing to maintain an efficient communication with them, valuable information is being lost.

To exemplify, consider the following initiatives: (a) the website PatientsLikeMe which facilitates the collection and analysis of patients' vital health indicators in relation to their medical interventions in order to disseminate these solutions to patients with similar illnesses; (b) Patient-innovation which is a website that offers a venue for patients to share and evaluate patient-developed solutions; and (c) Enablingthefuture.org, a collaborative community that develops customizable, modular, 3D-printable prosthetic hands.

As we evolve, so do the instruments and devices we use on a daily basis. Human beings are more connected to each other than ever through devices connected to the internet. This is known as the "Internet of things" (IOT), where a device is connected to the internet with an on and off switch. Nowadays, almost every device we can think off is being made with the capacity of being able to be connected and in communication with other devices. Some examples are: cellphones, laptops, tablets, watches, televisions, headphones, cars, airplanes and many more. The analyst firm Gartner says that by 2020 there will be over 26 billion connected devices worldwide (Morgan 2014).

The advantages of the use of the IOT on healthcare are countless and health care providers are incorporating them more and more on everyday activities either through services, therapeutically, for diagnosis and even for treatments. Chronic diseases and aging population are current and developing problems worldwide, the use of of IOT to control, treat and diagnose them are not only beneficial but efficient and usually less costly. For instance, the use of a continuous glucose monitoring (CGM) devices on diabetic patients are not only less laborious but more precise on monitoring glucose. Unlike a normal blood glucose meter that only provides a single glucose reading a CGM can provide information even every 5 min in real time. The GCM tracks glucose level through a sensor wire that is inserted to the skin and kept in place by an adhesive. Every time it reads a value it sends it to the receiver and the information can be read in real-time in the device or through an app. This data registration is not only useful to patients and their caregivers but also to their healthcare providers as it gives an insight on the patient's glucose levels and historical trends in levels (Dexcom continuous glucose monitoring 2019). Studies have shown that some CGM systems may help reduce A1C levels and reduce the risk for hypoglycemia, whether users are on insulin injections or pump therapy (Šoupal et al. 2016). Some devices are also able to alert the patient whether they are approaching a low or high glucose value during the day or even during the night and this way diminishing the risk of complications and even death. Physicians can then get the information from the device and look at trends and patterns of the patient's glucose levels to analyze current or future treatments. These type of devices help patients know how their glucose levels are at all times and can help physicians better decide a patient's treatment.

Along with the GCM, Closed Loop (automated) Insulin Delivery devices are now being used to detect glucose levels and then deliver the amount of insulin necessary and therefore "closing the loop". OpenAps is an example of this system, started in 2015 by Dana Lewis and her husband Scott Leibrand. He hacked her insulin pump in order to convert it into an automated pump by using the information her CGM provided. This technological system is now available and free for whoever has compatible medical devices and is willing to build their own system (Lewis 2015–2019). Earlier in 2013, Bryan Mazlish father and husband of diabetic patients with Type 1 Diabetes created a Closed-loop artificial pancreas device. He founded the SmartLoop Labs which is now known as Bigfoot Biomedical and are working to have a commercial launch of their system by 2020 which will hopefully be available worldwide and approved by the FDA (Bigfoot Biomedical 2019).

Many more devices and solutions are widely available for physicians and patients to use. Some of them are: CYCORE: a Bluetooth-enabled weight scale and blood pressure cuff, together with a symptom-tracking app used to send updates of patient's symptoms and responses to treatment to the physicians every weekday. Propeller Health and connected inhalers for asthma, which has a sensor that attaches to an inhaler or Bluetooth spirometer. It is then connected to an app that helps patients understand what can be causing their symptoms, allergen forecasts and track uses of rescue medication. Ingestible pill sensors made by Proteus Digital Health that dissolve in the stomach and send small signals to a sensor worn on the body stating that a patient has taken their medication. The Apple Watch to monitor depression by making the users monitor their moods and cognition on a daily basis. Although it has only been used in a pilot, it demonstrated to be useful giving both patients and healthcare professionals an insight of their condition. Apple watches have also been used to monitor Parkinson's Disease symptoms (10 Examples of the Internet of Things in Health Care 2019).

The IOT has permitted many new devices to be developed and used on a daily basis for the patient's benefit and to facilitate the reading of data done by physicians. Although they are now used by some, there is hope that these devices will be available and part of treatments worldwide for all. Devices can be used to wake a patient up, remind them to take a medication, to eat, to initiate physical activity and even to go to sleep. These devices not only make tracking of diseases easier, but also diminish costs for medical visits and make patients active actors of their health care.

3.6 Conclusions

In the last years, the number of publications that have been done about empowering patients and allowing them to take an active role and be engaged has been growing. It has been internationally identified as a key factor in the drives to improve health service delivery and quality (Barello et al. 2012). Patient engagement has three main variables that play important roles in the partnership. Firstly, the patient itself and the way they perceive their own needs and health status, their motivations and ability to engage, and lastly their beliefs and education. Their previous experiences can play a big role on whether or not they decide to open up or to share information about their lives. Some patients can belong to populations that are minorities and make it more challenging for them to feel fully integrated. Some of these vulnerable populations can be: people with disabilities, elderly, poor, low literacy, socioeconomically disadvantaged, children, refugees, limited language proficiency, racial and ethnic minorities.

The way a patient feels involved with their community and their health care organizations can influence the way they perceive others and the way they decide to share what they feel. Secondly, the health care institution can influence the ability of a patient to engage and communicate. Previous experiences with the hospital or clinic, previous encounters with the healthcare providers that work there and comments heard about the institution can influence a patient's desire to become engaged. If a hospital, for example, is not welcoming, restrictive with visiting hours, has cold nurses, uncomfortable waiting areas and bad food and is well known for these, patients will be reluctant to becoming engaged.

Lastly, the social aspect cannot be unseen as social norms and customs define who we are and how we act. If patients feel part of their communities and are not alienated, their willingness to take an active role will be increased. Patient engagement is the path towards cost reduction, quality improvement and more efficient services. To make the transition from a paternalistic medicine in which the provider has most of the power into a more patient centered service physicians' culture has to change. Along with the culture, the processes also have to have some changes in order to adapt into more patient centered services. Change takes time and sometimes needs trial and error. By taking into account a patient's outlook, a more fair, human and inclusive medicine can be practiced.

A patient comes to a healthcare professional and an organization and brings with him a tail made up of family and/or caregivers. It's important to take this into account as they are all indirect receptors and givers of information. It's through a patient's close social circle and a partnership with health care providers that health education and innovative approaches can be developed.

The greatest innovations have not only involved the patient but their supporters, who are generally their close family and friends. Patients who feel satisfied are more likely to express their feelings, concerns, doubts and ideas. They might do so, directly with health professionals or through patient experience platforms. It is important to be aware of all of the platforms patients choose to share their experiences, to make a better use of their suggestions and the feedback they provide. Patients and their families, health care professionals at all levels (ex. clinicians, administrators, members of professional societies, and researchers) as well as policy makers have all an important role in health care delivery. It's through their partnering that patients and their families will feel supported (Babiker et al. 2014). All benefit through a proper patient innovation input on health care, not only does it reduce research costs but also trial and error as patients themselves will have done it previously to sharing their successful innovation. Times are changing and so is the healthcare system, more focus should be done on patients and their needs, together the patients, caregivers and physicians can help reshape the system into a more reciprocal feedback approach.

References

10 Examples of the Internet of Things in Health Care. Ecoconsultancy. (2019). Retrieved from https://econsultancy.com/internet-of-things-healthcare/

Amann, J., Zanini, C., & Rubinelli, S. (2016). What online user innovation communities can teach us about capturing the experiences of patients living with chronic health conditions. A scoping review. *PLoS One, 11*(6), e0156175. https://doi.org/10.1371/journal.pone.0156175.

Arnstein, S. R. (November, 2007). A ladder of citizen participation. *Journal of the American Planning Association, 35*(4), 216–224.

Babiker, A., El Husseini, M., Al Nemri, A., Al Frayh, A., Al Juryyan, N., Faki, M. O., & Al Zamil, F. (2014). Health care professional development: Working as a team to improve patient care. *Sudanese Journal of Paediatrics, 14*(2), 9–16.

Barello, S., Graffigna, G., & Vegni, E. (2012). Patient engagement as an emerging challenge for healthcare services: Mapping the literature. *Nursing Research and Practice, 2012*, 905934. https://doi.org/10.1155/2012/905934.

Bigfoot Biomedical. (2019). Retrieved from https://www.bigfootbiomedical.com/about/faq

Bullinger-Hoffmann, A., Rass, M., Adamczyk, S., Moeslein, K., & Sohn, S. (2012). Open innovation in health care: Analysis of an open health platform. *Health Policy (Amsterdam, Netherlands), 105*, 165–175. https://doi.org/10.1016/j.healthpol.2012.02.009.

Carman, K. L., Dardess, P., Maurer, M., Sofaer, S., et al. (2013). Patient and family engagement: A framework For understanding the elements and developing interventions and policies. *Health Affairs, 32*(2), 223–231. Project HOPE—The People-to-People Health Foundation, Inc.

CE marking approval for medical devices in Europe. Medical devices. (2019). *BSI group*. Retrieved from https://www.bsigroup.com/en-US/medical-devices/Our-services/CE-marking/

Chesbrough, H. W. (2003). *Open innovation: The new imperative for creating and profiting from technology*. Boston, MA: Harvard Business School Press.

Dexcom Continuous Glucose Monitoring. (2019). Retrieved from https://www.dexcom.com/continuous-glucose-monitoring

Frampton, S., & Patrick, A. C. (2008). *Putting patients first: Best practices in patient-centered care* (2nd ed.). San Francisco: Jossey-Bass Publishers.

Fursov, K., Thurner, T., & Nefedova, A. (2017). What user-innovators do that others don't: A study of daily practices. *Technological Forecasting and Social Change*. https://doi.org/10.1016/j.techfore.2017.02.016.

Habicht, H., Oliveira, P., & Shcherbatiuk, V. (2012, August 27). User innovators: When patients set out to help themselves and end up helping many. *Die Unternehmung, 66*(3), 277–294. Available at SSRN from https://ssrn.com/abstract=2144325

Kaplan, A. L., Cohen, E. R., & Zimlichman, E. (2017). Improving patient engagement in self-measured blood pressure monitoring using a mobile health technology. *Health Information Science and Systems, 5*(1), 4. https://doi.org/10.1007/s13755-017-0026-9.

Kilgas, R. (2018). *Medical Timeline. Time Graphics*. Retrieved from https://time.graphics/event/497942

Lewis, D. *OpenAps (2015-2019)*. Retrieved from https://openaps.org/

Lorenzo's Oil. The Myelin Project. (2018). Retrieved from https://www.myelin.org/lorenzos-oil/

Maffei, S., Bianchini, M., Parini, B., & Cipriani, L. (2019). *MakeToCare2. La patient innovation in Italia tra progetto e mercato*. Milano: Libraccio Editore.

Mc Namara, K. P., Versace, V. L., Marriott, J. L., & Dunbar, J. A. (2014, August). Patient engagement strategies used for hypertension and their influence on self-management attributes. *Family Practice, 31*(4), 437–444. https://doi.org/10.1093/fampra/cmu026.

Morgan, J. A simple explanation of 'The Internet of Things (2014). *Forbes*. Retrieved from https://www.forbes.com/sites/jacobmorgan/2014/05/13/simple-explanation-internet-things-that-any one-can-understand/#61582e4b1d09

My Runway of Dreams Story By Mindy Scheier. (2015). *Don't hide it, flaunt it. Celebrating a world of differences*. Retrieved from http://www.donthideitflauntit.com/runway-dream-post/

Oliveira, P., Zejnilovic, L., Canhão, H., & von Hippel, E. (2015). Innovation by patients with rare diseases and chronic needs. *Orphanet Journal of Rare Diseases, 10*, 41. https://doi.org/10.1186/s13023-015-0257-2.

Patient Engagement: Technical Series on Safer Primary Care. (2016). Geneva: World Health Organization. License: CC BY-NC-SA 3.0 IGO.

Patient-Reported Experience Measures (PREMS). (2015). *A scoping document to inform the evaluation of the NHS vanguard sites*. Yorkshire and Humber: Academic Health Science Network.

Patient-Reported Outcomes (PROs) assessment. (2019, May 20). *European Patients Academy (EUPATI)*. Retrieved from https://www.eupati.eu/clinical-development-and-trials/patient-reported-outcomes-pros-assessment/

Regulatory Controls for Medical Devices. (2018). *U.S. Food and Drug Administration*. Retrieved from https://www.fda.gov/medical-devices/overview-device-regulation/regulatory-controls

Scheier, M. *Blue Ocean-shift-strategy-leadership (2004-2019)*. Retrieved from https://www.blueoceanstrategy.com/community/blue-ocean-stories/mindy-scheier/

Schieir, M. (2016). *I launched a nonprofit to empower people with disabilities through adaptive clothing. TIME*. Retrieved from http://time.com/4232633/tommy-hilfiger-adaptive-clothing-run way-of-dreams/

Šoupal, J., Petruželková, L., Flekač, M., Pelcl, T., Matoulek, M., Daňková, M., & Prázný, M. (2016). Comparison of different treatment modalities for type 1 diabetes, including sensor-augmented insulin regimens, in 52 weeks of follow-up: A COMISAIR study. *Diabetes Technology & Therapeutics, 18*(9), 532–538. https://doi.org/10.1089/dia.2016.0171.

Spyropoulou, G. A., & Fatah, F.(2008). *Decorative tattooing for scar camouflage: Patient innovation*. Birmingham: Department of Plastic and Reconstructive Surgery, City Hospital. JPRAS.

Squeeze machine. (2019). *Therafin Corporation*. Retrieved from http://www.therafin.com/squeezemachine.htm

Temple Grandin. (1992). Calming effects of deep touch pressure in patients with autistic disorder, college students, and animals. *Journal of Child and Adolescent Psychopharmacology, 2*(1), 63–72.

The shower shirt Company. Lisa F. Crites. Our story. Retrieved from https://www.theshowershirt.com/our-story/

Weldring, T., & Smith, S. M. (2013). Patient-reported outcomes (PROs) and patient-reported outcome measures (PROMs). *Health Services Insights, 6*, 61–68. https://doi.org/10.4137/HSI.S11093.

What's the Difference Between the FDA Medical Device Classes? (2018). *BMP Medical. Creating medical solutions*. Retrieved from https://www.bmpmedical.com/blog/whats-difference-fda-medical-device-classes-2/

Wheat, H., et al. (2018). Can practitioners use patient reported measures to enhance person centred coordinated care in practice? A qualitative study. *Health and Quality of Life Outcomes*. https://doi.org/10.1186/s12955-018-1045-1.

Zejnilovic, L., Oliveira, P., & Canao, H. (2016). Innovations by and for patients, and their place in the future health care system. In H. Albach, H. Meffert, A. Pinkwart, R. Reichwald, & W. von Eiff (Eds.), *Boundaryless hospital*. Berlin: Springer.

Chapter 4
Cases of Patient Innovation

Abstract This chapter describes four case studies and the process innovators went through while developing their products. These case studies were chosen because they are linked to technological innovations. The Oncomfort Case is about implementation of virtual reality in a cancer hospital to reduce pain and anxiety in patients. The Tippytalk Platform Case, is a platform created by a father for his non-verbal autistic daughter so that she could communicate with others. The Open Sesame App Case is an Android app for patients with mobility disabilities, it uses the device's internal camera to track the user's face and uses their movements to control the screen. The Feelif is a social innovation developed to improve creativity in blind and visually impaired patients using technological devices, sounds and vibrations. Throughout the book several innovations have been mentioned, a variety of product innovations were chosen to expose the fact that, patient innovations can vary from a simple jean redesigning to an actual technological device.

Keywords Patient innovation · Caregivers · Case study research · Digital technology · Patient experience · Quality of care

4.1 Introduction

The aim of this chapter is to illustrate a number of successful cases of patient innovations from all around the world. As previously mentioned, patient innovations not only help solve existing problems concerning a patient's daily life challenges but also enrich the health care sector. Through their hard work, research, prototype development, trial and errors and constant improvements, innovative and necessary products are developed. It is easy to forget the gifts we have in front of our eyes; we might take for granted having sight, arms, mobility and health itself but patients who lack all of these and many more, have to find solutions to their limitations. It's through their feedback and innovations that health actors get to see the necessities and challenges patients have on a daily basis. Books can illustrate what a disease can look like but it's only through patients' experiences and anecdotes that we really

© The Author(s), under exclusive licence to Springer Nature Switzerland AG 2020   73
F. Schiavone, *User Innovation in Healthcare*, SpringerBriefs in Health Care
Management and Economics, https://doi.org/10.1007/978-3-030-44256-9_4

know what a burden it is to have a disease or a specific limitation. Thanks to brave and creative innovators, the world can now have medical innovative products that range in prices and quality.

Many focuses were selected on the development of this book. The process of product development was exposed in the first chapter as well as how customer input affects new service development processes, types of user innovations and user and Producer Innovation. On Chap. 2, the concept of health technology was further developed, its principles and proper assessment, innovation in healthcare, the patterns of it, its digitalization and the implications of this digitalization. Top healthcare innovations were also exposed and the role of users in the healthcare innovation. The author then decided to include in Chap. 3 an introduction to patient innovation and patient engagement and combined it with short explanations of patient innovations as well as the mechanism of diffusion of these innovations through social media. An open-source software Bibliometrix was also used via www.bibliometrix.org and www.bibliometrix.com following these steps: (1) identification of the key themes; (2) research design; (3) data collection; (4) data analysis; (5) data visualization; (6) data interpretation with descriptive statistics, data reduction techniques or mappings. Finally, the author decided to include four case studies in the present chapter to make the patient innovation process more comprehensible and to have a better understanding of the topic. In this chapter, some cases will be explained in detail so you can get to see the process of a product innovation, the development and the final steps of the process. The cases fully expanded later on in this chapter are all related to technology usage. We can't deny the takeover of technology in our daily lives, therefore these cases were chosen.

4.2   Research Method

There are various ideas about what a case study is. According to scholars that are experts in the topic a case study should have a case that is related to the topic of study. It should be approached with multiple methods, be contemporary and have multiple functioning units that make it easy to digest and relate to (Yin 2009; Miles et al. 1994). It should be able to accentuate different features related to the research topic. Some argue that the techniques used to investigate and find a proper case study are not as important as it is to find a case that actually complements the research topic (Robert Stake 2005). Others think that the method used to research for an adequate case study is more important (Robert Yin 2009).

Multiple case studies are further developed in this chapter to better comprehend the process and development of patient innovation and the impact of patient engagement in the process. As recommended by Yin (2009), multiple sources of data were used to construct validity from official documents and statistics to personal interviews. The author focused his work on patient innovation because of the great impact it is having in healthcare. Although it is a very apparent and ongoing phenomenon, this type of innovation is still not fully acknowledged in many countries. In recent years the interest has been growing but more exposure is still needed. Illustrative case studies make it easier to understand the process of a given phenomenon and has a detailed description on the development of the innovation, in this case. Not only is it useful in exposing the chronological steps but also makes the reader more relatable to the process and can challenge the current data available on patient innovation or open a new interest on the topic.

4.3 Case Studies

4.3.1 Oncomfort

Cancer is one of the most common leading causes of death in the world (Bray et al. 2018). It refers to any one of a large number of diseases characterized by the development of abnormal cells that divide uncontrollably and have the ability to infiltrate, spread to other parts of the body and destroy normal body tissue. In addition, cancer can have a severe impact on psychosocial wellbeing on not only the patient but also their environment (Mayo Clinic staff, Oct. 4 2018). More specifically, pain and anxiety occur not only due to the disease itself, but are also treatment-related, for example during hospital procedures. Psychological stress is part of the lives of human beings, but prolonged exposure to it can reduce the quality of life (National Cancer Institute 2012). As such, experiencing anxiety can be regarded as the most common psychiatric disorder (Mavridou et al. 2013; Remes et al. 2018). Similarly, pain is the most reported complaint in the medical world and has a negative impact on the healing process and hospital admittance rates (National Center for Health Statistics 2006).

Diane Jooris is a 47 years old Belgian innovator. She has master degrees in clinical psychology, international relations and laws. Before starting her own company, she used to work as a hypnosis specialist in oncology at MD Anderson Cancer Centre in Texas. Her passion lies within yoga training and taking time for her children. Diane Jooris is the CEO and co-founder of the Oncomfort® company (Oncomfort 2017; Van Steenkist 2018). Since the diagnosis of both her father and her sister, Diane decided she wanted to ease the pain experiences her family was going through. It was very frustrating for her to watch other people suffer, especially her family. By doing her job, Diane saw other patients freaking out before chemo sessions and operations. She is very passionate about helping cancer patients throughout their journey. Her goal was to help them in this process and make them feel more relaxed. Because of the support and good practices gained from her sister, Diane decided to go on with her psychological support. Therefore, she combined her clinical hypnosis expertise with the rise of a new technology, namely virtual reality. As a mental health professional, her focus is set on pain and anxiety reduction of cancer patients (Oncomfort 2017; Van Steenkist 2018).

As has been stated earlier, anxiety and pain are significant burdens of disease all around the world. There are many effective ways to reduce or eliminate anxiety and pain in individuals, but the problem is that these conditions are not often recognized or treated effectively (Remes et al. 2018). In addition, experiencing this distress in a hospital environment seems to have become normal (Mavridou et al. 2013). Just like anxiety, the most common but most expensive treatment of pain is pharmaceuticals (Cherny et al. 2001; Hoffman et al. 2006). However, pharmaceuticals only have a limited effect as cancer patients experience constant distress which is characterized by mental, social, emotional or spiritual suffering (National Cancer Institute 2012). Thus, it is clear that there is an unmet need for cancer patients as there often is a lack of comprehensive efforts in mitigating psychological treatment-related stress. Cancer patients should also be taught how to manage these negative feelings with techniques such as breathing and relaxation therapy, counseling, social support and physical exercise. In the recent years, cost-effective and innovative diversion mechanism such as virtual reality has gained increasing attention (Kindler et al. 2000; Ramamohan et al. 2018).

Virtual Reality is a term that got more and more attention in our society in the last several years. The spectacles in which you escape from the real world and are brought to a virtual reality are no longer unknown for the people in this world. The application was recently used in the world of video games in which large companies such as Google and Nintendo came up with innovative models on the market. Today, virtual reality eyewear is also given a purpose in the medical world. After studies in different settings in the hospital environment, the devices appear to have their effect on different areas (Pandya et al. 2017; Pourmand et al. 2018).

The distraction of the patient can be done in an active or passive way. The passive distraction of the patient can be by the means of audio equipment that allows the patient to hear music or, for example, by watching images on a screen (Prabhakar et al. 2007). An active form of distraction is the typical example of 'virtual reality distraction' in which the patient actively participates and effectively escapes the reality (Nilsson et al. 2009). This way of distraction can remove pain and anxiety to a much greater extent than the passive form can (Guo et al. 2015). In addition to the studies on the effectiveness of virtual reality in a hospital environment, studies whether the content of the images can have an influence on the patient were also reviewed. These can be very different and seem to affect the patient's perception to some extent (Tanja-Dijkstra et al. 2018). The virtual reality glasses also seem to be a good application for therapies to remove phobias. Research showed the effectiveness of the use of images in virtual reality glasses on reducing anxiety on patients (Miloff et al. 2016).

Currently, the company has a lot of different types of systems. The first virtual reality program they created was called 'Aqua' used for relaxation and for the self-management of the patient. The patient experiences a water environment which causes relaxation. Another project is 'AMO' and this is used during clinical procedures and procedures under local anesthesia. 'Kimo' is the personal favorite of Diane Jooris. This type of virtual reality provides education to children who will undergo chemotherapy. The video explains in a very simple and animated way how everything works and what will happen. It provides then them a nice learning experience and some distraction. 'Spacio' is also created for children and gives them an anti-anxiety treatment before undergoing MRI or radiotherapy. The last project is also made for children, this is the 'Stella' project and can be used during small procedures done in children.

The success of virtual reality in the 'gaming world' suggests that it could have its advantages in other sectors, such as the medical sector. Virtual Reality can achieve a reduction of anxiety and pain because the attention of the patient is diverted. A person can only give a limited degree of conscious attention to a certain stimulus and experiencing pain demands that conscious attention. The removal of this conscious attention by giving a patient the feeling of being in a different reality ensures that the pain is felt in a smaller degree. This reduced feeling of pain therefore causes a reduction in anxiety (Hoffman et al. 2004). Research even shows that patients can experience a sense of pleasure during the virtual reality experience (Schmitt et al. 2011). Furthermore, the use of VR could improve current practices characterized with an over-usage of pain medications, which are associated with adverse side effects, such as: nausea, vomiting, itching, constipation, urinary retention, but also respiratory problems, addiction or excessive sedation (Cherny et al. 2001; Hoffman et al. 2006).

As stated, cancer (treatment) leads to anxiety and pain and if the patient wears the VR goggles and listens to the audio during the treatment, he can't be fully focused on the pain and anxiety. It immerses the conscious attention to the VR experience. During the try-out versions, the results were promising. The patients responded well to the treatment and suffered less pain and anxiety. This positive influence has also been seen in dental visits, where patients have the feeling that they are at another location, consequently reducing anxiety and pain among adults and children (Aminabadi et al. 2012; Al-Khotani et al. 2016). A second example is in the care of patients with burn wounds. In this specific area, test subjects do not only have a lower degree of pain during a treatment, but also the use of pain medication is significantly lower (Hoffman et al. 2004; Ebrahimi et al. 2018). A last successful application is in the treatment of chronic pain in which there is a prolonged process of not only physical pain, but also an interplay of psychological aspects (Guarino et al. 2017). It is apparent that this innovative form of pain and anxiety reduction can therefore be used at different settings in a hospital for improving the experiences of different patient groups.

The first step of the innovation process was the feeling of frustration of Diane Jooris in trying to reduce cancer patients' anxiety during stressful procedures or before surgeries. According to Diane, significant time has to be spent on the patient in person to reduce anxiety, but this was not always possible due to time constraints. Because of her experiences she endeavoured to find solutions, of which a newly developed audio solution was her first idea. This audio solution consisted of a library of standardized psychological sessions. Although there were some positive effects on the patient's anxiety, they were not enough for Diana. It was during this stage of the innovation that Joowon Kim got involved and a virtual reality solution was determined as the missing piece. This innovation addressed the issues of limited time the staff had and the difficulty in helping the patients in real time. Over time, VR made it possible to execute operations without bringing the patients in full narcosis, but more often under local anaesthesia. This way, potential harmful effects of narcosis are avoided.

This innovative process started with cancer patients but Diana extended her therapy to other diagnostic groups. At first it was difficult to convince doctors of the benefits of using this product during procedures. In addition, finding partners was quite troublesome. However, at this moment Oncomfort® has established durable relationships with several cancer institutions in Europe and research centers in the United States, Belgium Italy, Lebanon, Ecuador and the United Kingdom.

Oncomfort® distinguishes themselves for their availability and prompt response to people that contact them. They are widely available in social media and through their online website. Their Twitter account is @oncomfort, which they use to easily interact with their followers by posting pictures, articles and general information on their products. Diane Jooris also has a personal twitter account @dianejooris where she shares relevant information about Oncomfort and their achievements. Oncomfort can also be found on Instagram as: @oncomfortsa but they are not that active in this platform, with only one to six posts a month. Furthermore, the company can be found on Linkedin as Oncomfort with a brief explanation about their company and the employees whom are listed in their information box. In Facebook they have an accessible page: @oncomfortsa, yet with only 514 followers at the time of consulting. Moreover, their official website is hosted at oncomfort.com, where you can obtain the latest updates. Additionally, videos concerning patients' experiences, medical procedures in which their goggles are being used, medical doctors explaining the benefits of using VR and small clips of the digital graphics the patients can experience can be viewed on their channel on YouTube. Oncomfort has also been featured in many newspapers and health websites around the world.

Diane Jooris founded the company with her own savings. Later, she had financial support from friends, family, business angels and other donations. By the end of 2017, Oncomfort® was launched commercially and the testing phase in France and Belgium was closed. Its employees have multiple ethnicity backgrounds and are multilingual, it is a very international group of dynamic people. They are all scattered around the world and can be found in: Europe, North America, South America and Asia. Oncomfort's® headquarters are based in Brussels, Belgium but do active research and development in other countries as well.

The program is currently available in eight languages: English, French, Spanish, Portuguese, Italian, German, Arabic and Dutch. There used to be an office in the United States, but they realised they were missing the real market in Europe. At the moment they are focused on expansion of the company in Europe, but the ambition of going back to America is still present. Within their strategy, physicians using the technology are the key component. They report on the benefits from VR treatments to their colleagues, widening the market for Oncomfort® itself. In order to expand the company even more, Oncomfort is seeking collaborations with leading cancer institutions, pharma-companies and foundations. Some associations have been already been achieved with medical cancer institutions in Europe and research centres in the United States, Belgium, Italy, Lebanon, Ecuador and the United Kingdom.

The VR therapy is sold to surgeons, anaesthesiologists and any kind of doctor performing anxiety or pain treatments. The VR glasses are sold for 740 euro a piece, without any profit for Oncomfort. They also offer a software which is activated through a monthly payment. The client can also receive clinical and technical support. This is where the company gains profit out of their service. It is optional to subscribe for only one accompanying game or to subscribe to the whole Oncomfort library. It is also possible for the patients to gain a reimbursement from insurance companies on the use of the device.

Currently, the virtual reality program is only available for patients in the hospital setting in which one session comprises 18 min before a surgery or other treatments. There are already great results but the goal is to further increase the number of programs that can be offered to include different issues and diseases. In the future it could be possible for doctors to prescribe virtual reality as a type of anxiety treatment. Telemedicine is already growing for medical procedures, but can also be used in the future for mental health care as well. Another goal of Oncomfort® is to cover the whole cancer journey, from diagnosis to treatment and beyond. The company wants to be there in every key stage a cancer patient and their caregivers go through. Many people in Europe are ready for this innovative device, in Northern-America however, the process of introducing the Oncomfort® therapy is a bit difficult. This is due to the many influences of pharmaceutical companies, limiting the expected popularity. The company is still hopeful, declaring that many Europeans are already asking for similar therapies in North-America. Therefore, Oncomfort® has established a partnership with the University of Texas with the main goal to gain popularity.

4.3.2 The Tippytalk

Autism is a neuro-developmental disorder, characterized by several symptoms. The term "Autistic Spectrum Disorders" (ASD) has been introduced just in recent years. Its symptoms appear mostly between the first 6 months and the two/three years of life of the child; they are usually noticed by the parents, and they can increase in severity throughout the years; sometimes irreversible. ASD usually compromises the development of social interactions and communication skills of the sufferers and causes limited, repetitive and/or stereotyped behaviours, which can also result in compulsive and self-injurious attitudes. Though even today we do not know what its etiopathogenesis is, scientists hypothesize different causes, including some genetic and environmental ones (e.g. maternal nutritional factors, atmospheric pollution, etc.). Some of the various syndromes of ASD are the Asperger's syndrome, the Rett's syndrome and the disintegrative disorder of childhood.

Rob Laffan is a 41-year-old Irish Robotic engineer and Sadie's dad, an 8-year-old autistic girl: he created TippyTalk, an app for autistic children. He firstly attended the "Christian Brothers School Limerick", from 1982 to 1995. Then, he finished high school with average results and he did not go to the university or college. From 1995 to 2010 Rob had a lot of different jobs, amongst them are: factory floor worker, Post-Man, Courier Sales officer and even an Auto-Mechanic Pizza deliverer. He was also active in the manufacturing floor of computer companies, like Dell and Samsung, so he is very used to working with ICT systems. He was then a manager of a motors department, in charge of looking after projects of new vehicles and engines. Just before creating TippyTalk, he was a pharmaceutical sales agent, delivering medicines to pharmacies, hospitals and, more generally, to Healthcare (HC) providers. This experience made him very much familiar with the commercial needs of such HC delivery organizations.

In 2010, Sadie was born and Rob had just lost his job as a pharmaceutical sales person. In 2012, due to the need of improving his economic conditions and supporting his family, he decided to go back to education and he started attending the faculty of Industrial Engineering Automation and Robotic Systems at the Limeric Institute of Technology. A few weeks later, his wife Emily and himself realized that something was wrong with Sadie and in the way, she was growing up: within a year, she had gotten a diagnosis of non-verbal autism.

After receiving this hard news, Rob decided to do something concrete with the technology he was studying at the time. Before Tippy Talk, Sadie was very frustrated and she frequently had problems when sleeping and was very quiet. Indeed, the real reason why Rob invented the platform was to help Sadie communicate her emotions, her needs and her desires. This made it easier for her to communicate beyond the confinement of her room, without distance being a problem or a limitation. In addition, as Sadie grows up, the app will allow her to communicate with her friends and peers, giving her the opportunity to approach and improve her social life through technology, above all during this time of technological revelation, in the same way all other teenagers do (e.g. through Facebook or Instagram).

In 2015 Rob completed his Bachelor degree in Engineering and he followed several certified programs in non-verbal communication for children and adults. He soon came up with the idea of building the TippyTalk, in 2014, which was then tested in 2015. Its app version was created in 2016. Moreover, he won the International Automation Student Innovation Award in 2014, due to TippyTalk. As well as the Student entrepreneur of the year award (National Award) Enterprise Ireland and the Student engineer of the year award (National Award) Engineers Ireland in 2015. From June 2015 to February 2016 he attended the Enterprise Ireland Entrepreneur boot camp (New Frontiers). In 2016 Rob created a company based in Ireland and US, with a staff of 10–15 people and a SaaS (Software-as-a-Service) business model.

Before Rob's innovation, some incumbent technologies or products providing care for such specific illness already existed, but they did not address the ability for a non-verbal person to communicate beyond the boundaries of the room they were in. Among these technologies there are the AssistiveWare apps, which help children, teens and adults who cannot speak, through the use of symbol and text-based support for daily communication. Therefore, they are built to fulfil the user's needs, including visual and motor skill impairments. AssistiveWare communication solutions are: Proloquo2Go (a daily communication tool to build language skills), Proloquo4Text (to confidently communicate), Pictello app (to create and share visual stories and schedules), Keeble app (to type in almost any iOS app easier and faster for people with physical and vision impairments).

Another incumbent technology is the assistive Tobii Dynavox, a robust hardware, helping in augmentative and alternative communication (using devices, systems and techniques), in the attempt of communicating more effectively in the same room, despite significant communication challenges. The main difference between these two incumbent technologies and TippyTalk concerns the cost, because these apps are two specific image communication tools used in a same room, and they respectively cost $300 and $6000. On the other hand, TippyTalk is for outside room communication—thus global—providing customized images and costing $100 per year.

TippyTalk is a platform that helps people with verbal disability to socially integrate themselves. The basic idea is to involve them, above all during the actual technological era, in using new means to express their own feelings, emotions, likes and dislikes. The aim is that of transmitting a sort of "technologically equality", according to which technology must be available to everyone, regardless to your ability or disability. TippyTalk is a picture-based communication system, that enables people with verbal disability to instantly connect with anyone, anywhere and anytime. It is a 3-step communicating software:

1. Select who you want to talk to, by selecting an image of the person;
2. Select what you want to talk about (by choosing a category and then a specific object);
3. Send the message.

TippyTalk EDU is now being developed, which is a step up from the TippyTalk. The main differences between TippyTalk and TippyTalkEDU is that the first app is based on a "one-way" communication system—where messages are delivered by SMS to the caregiver's phone—while the second one works on a "two-way app to app" communication system, just like WhatsApp or Facebook messenger. TippyTalkEDU (launched in January 2019) has a back-end web analytic centre, that captures communication data from the app, it then delivers more and more improved custom reports to professionals, especially in the education system.

The innovation process has been specifically developed through the following 11 consecutive steps:

1. Developing the proof of concept;
2. Testing the proof of concept to debug, i.e. making the programmer identify and correct one or more errors (bugs) detected in the software and enhancing performance;
3. Submitting to the Irish patent office, for short-term world-wide patent protection for 2 years;
4. Submitting to the patent office of chosen countries, for full patent protection;
5. Embarking on raising capital and finance;
6. Securing capital and finance;

7. Getting government backing;
8. Picking target market, carefully paying close attention to those who need it to talk and communicate;
9. Picking in location;
10. Delivering to the market;
11. Scaling the product to reduce the cost of the app.

Each step was fundamental for the innovator in the development of the app, for legal, academic and personal reasons. The biggest challenge Rob faced was not about the creation of the app itself, but the steps of figuring out this type of innovation, from the touchscreen to a valid interaction with the operative system, in order to provide excellent communication. Originally, TippyTalk had six different interactions, which later became four, and lastly three, thanks to Sadie's help and feedback. Rob created the first original version of the app by himself, but also with the help of Limerick Ireland, an Irish developers' company. This company is located in the same city as Rob and can be considered his first official partner.

Rob and his team have created an analytic portal specifically for TippyTalkEDU, where all data can be sent back and forth. This data is systematically collected and monitored. Indeed, for the second version, he has outsourced this kind of service to a company called "Magic Software", based in New York, but supported by the team of developers in Delhi, who are also the developers of TippyTalkEDU and current partners. He however finds it quite challenging to work with them from time to time. Firstly, because of a considerable time difference. Secondly, because even though they are very fluent in English, there is still some significant loss of information in translation (e.g. they can assume different meanings for a given word, thus making its translation completely inappropriate). For this reason, especially during the development process, it could be better to pick someone as close as possible and with the same language: all this can cost more, in the immediate term, but it can also save a lot of money in the long term, mostly for what concerns communication, which is basically one of the main challenges to face nowadays.

The first interview made to Rob led to a viral video, which got 350 million views, 750,000 shares and 75,000 downloads in just 2 weeks. The revenue generated from this, allowed him to build TippyTalkEDU. Social media has played an important role in the development and constant updating of the app. Facebook for example, is very useful for the promotion of the app as it is one of the most important advertising platforms nowadays. Moreover, the innovation has expanded thanks to the creation of the official website (www.tippy-talk.com), in which instructions to download the app can be found. There are videos on the website that help explain the use of the app; these are also found on YouTube. Furthermore, a specific part of the website, named "Testimonials", is dedicated to the testimonies of those who have already used the app and their positive feedbacks, as well as ideas for future improvements. In particular, you can find impactful parents' testimonies about the first time their autistic children used the app and were able to communicate with them. Descriptive testimonies point out the way the app has helped autistic children express what they want, their needs, and the way it has impacted and changed their lives.

Table 4.1 Affordable subscription prices

Country	Subscription price per quarter	Subscription price per year
United States	$ 42.99 US	$ 99.99 US
Canada	$ 55.99 CA	$ 134.99 CA
Australia	$ 65.99 AU	$ 154.99 AU
United Kingdom	£ 33.99	£ 97.99
Belgium, Finland, France, Germany, Italy, Ireland, Netherlands, Portugal, Spain	€ 44.99	€ 99.99
Norway	445,00 kr NO	1090.00 kr NO
Sweden	489,00 kr SE	1149.00 kr SE
Denmark	349,00 kr DK	889.00 kr DK

Source: Our elaboration

TippyTalk is currently used by more than 3500 individuals in more than 50 different countries (84% from the US), which is really relevant, considering the actual exponential growth of the worldwide market size of more than 500 million non-verbal sufferers. After offering the availability of benefiting from a one-month free trial, TippyTalk app actually requires a subscription to be used. By the end of the trial, users are prompted to do the following steps: Provide credit card information—depending on the policy of the given app store on trial and app download payment—i.e. charging it to personal iTunes, Googleplay or Android accounts, getting an automatic renewal within 24 hrs, prior to the end of the current subscription period, unless auto-renewal is disabled beforehand, selecting the option to have the subscription automatically renewed quarterly/yearly, etc. Finally, once the purchase is done, they have the possibility to manage their own personal subscription and can disable the auto-renewal payment whenever.

The affordable subscription prices are reported below (Table 4.1), both in quarterly and yearly terms and also include the costs of SMS' sent—which vary from country to country—whose amount is however with no limits comprised in the subscription price of TippyTalk.

The competitive context which we are actually dealing with is the one of growing app creators and, in general, ICT entrepreneurs, finally putting their attention on the ASD community. In particular, all these actors are trying to focalize on a sort of "middle earth" between the provision of developmental and communication aids and the accomplishment of learning the needs of autistic children. By adopting an educational perspective, what emerges from the current state of the art, is nothing but a quite strict need for accessible apps. These are based on visual hints and encouraging tools, that could also help in clearly defining students' daily schedules. At the same time, these devices would continue to assist autistic children throughout the years through their development. This would help detect and make improvements in the apps to better identify and regulate emotions, express themselves, calmly manage routine activities and successfully experience social exchanges.

In the attempt of satisfying all these incumbent expectations, the next goal TippyTalk has is that of applying into the K12 special needs school districts of the

US and hopefully worldwide. Meanwhile, the company is in fact rolling out a specific educational package, based on a license, for teachers, assistants and pupils, able to work on observable metrics, which can in turn be analysed by teachers and therapists, with the aim of assessing individual progress, determining whether he/she is requiring more/less learning assistance, but also delivering world class communication and effective educational methods.

This kind of "disruptive" solution is without a doubt able to ensure continuous monitoring and updating of the mental status, to improve efforts from time to time, for reducing the problems that arise to non-verbal sufferers, when trying to communicate with others. In the light of the above mentioned, this is ultimately important in terms of prevention, especially speaking of young adults in teaching environments, as these situations can lead to violent acts, for which teachers cannot intervene and might end up calling authorities.

4.3.3 Open Sesame

Spinal injuries are some of the most complex pathologies studied in the medical world. The spinal column, or vertebral column holds and protects the spinal cord, which, is the main part of the central nervous system. Composed of nerves it is in charge of sending sensitive and motor signals throughout the body to the brain and back. The cervical region, referred to as C1 through C7, control signals to the neck, arms, hands, and, in some cases, the diaphragm. When this area is injured it can cause tetraplegia, or as it is more commonly called quadriplegia amongst many other affections. Multiple sclerosis (MS) is an autoimmune-mediated disease in which an abnormal response of the body's immune system is directed against the central nervous system (CNS). Given the fact it affects the CNS, signs and symptoms can vary in location and also in intensity. It can affect the optic nerves, the extremities, and much more. Patients with MS usually encounter mobility problems, fatigue, visual disturbances, altered sensation and more.

Oded Ben-Dov is the CTO and the co-founder of the app "Open Sesame", he is a far-sighted innovator and a fluent speaker of 11 languages, two spoken and nine programming. He has always been fond of working with computers, starting from the Commodore 64 (a very old computer), up to the recent IOs applications development. He studied in Israel, lived in Canada for 2 years as a kid and did a mandatory military service in Israel after. When he left the army, he started working in the high tech business and completed a computer science degree from which he graduated with Summa cum laude at the Israel Institute of Technology.

Oded usually worked with games and apps that used the camera a lot, one day he received a phone call from a person that was unable to use his hands and legs, asking for a way to use his smartphone. That person is the actual co-founder of the "Open Sesame" app, he is called Giora Livne and is an electrical power engineer, with a large experience in the management of intricate systems and construction of high-tech assembly lines. Giora became quadriplegic after an accident, he is the inspiration for the creation of Sesame Enable. Oded got the idea from a computer app that uses the mechanism of waving the hands and the head to enable certain commands. He is a strong promoter for life-changing, technological solutions for people with physical challenges. The meeting with Giova changed his vision of the utilization of high-tech technologies, he understood the importance that his knowledge could bring to people with disabilities. Furthermore, with the implementation of this app, he realized the scarcity of prototypes, projects, information and applications that can lead to a more harmonious cohabitation of these people with their own disability and with the rest of the world.

Before the launch of the Sesame app in 2012, a similar computer program already existed. This freeware, is known as the NPointer, it is a PC gestural control system that recognizes hand movements and translates them into mouse- pointer movements. It can be used in two different ways: If the webcam is external to the PC, for example on USB, it could be pointed directly on the back of the hand that could move freely on the desk. If instead the webcam is integrated into the computer, as in laptops, to move the mouse pointer the users have to move the palm of the hand in front of the webcam, with the back facing their face. It is also possible to activate mouse commands with head movements, to do so it is necessary to put a check mark on the Head/frontal control option and move the head in front of the webcam to move the pointer where the user wants it to move.

In 2016, 4 years later after the launch of the Sesame app, thanks to the economic financing of the Spanish Vodafone Foundation, an app, known as EVA Facial Mouse, was developed by CREA Sistemas Informaticos. The app is available for free on the Google Play Store but has only been adapted for a limited number of Android devices. The app uses the device's internal camera to track the user's face and based on the movement of the face, allows the user to control a pointer (mouse) on the screen. The cursor can touch any item on the screen and can be used to navigate the phone interface. In order to be able to do a click the procedure is very simple: the cursor needs to be kept over the part of the screen the user wants to activate. Furthermore, it includes a menu that allows easy access to the main functions of the device. This application has significant limitations due to limited access to most user interface elements. It cannot be used with all browsers, it works best in Google Chrome and it has not been tested with all devices on the market.

Despite the different similar technologies available, none is comparable to the Sesame app. It manages to reduce the technological gap and to improve the quality of life of disabled people (overcoming the problem and being able to use the devices), a very important goal especially in a society like ours where smartphones and tablets have become essential for everyone. 'Open Sesame' is an Android app which can be downloaded in the Google Play Store and enables users to control any app without touching the screen. It is available only for Android systems because the IOs system doesn't allow the app to customize the device. It is the first app that allows people with hand disabilities to use their smartphone with a technology similar to the one that was previously available for computers with special cameras that were used to track the head movements. The users are mostly patients who are paralyzed below the neck.

The app can be enabled by saying "Ok Google", this can work either if the screen is locked or not. Then the user must say "Open Sesame" so the app can be opened. There is also an option to open the app directly by saying "Open Sesame". The device's camera works by tracking the user's head movements. These tracked movements are combined with cutting-edge computer vision algorithms to create a cursor that appears on the screen of the phone, like the cursor on a computer screen. The on-screen cursor is controlled by the position and movements of a user's head and can even detect minimal movements. The app can be customized, for instance choosing the point sensitivity of the neck movement to control the cursor. Commands like tap or swipe, can be used through an interactive menu. It can be activated by moving the cursor in any part of the screen and waiting for about 2 seconds or the time it takes for the green line around the cursor to complete its cycle. Then a menu appears and displays four possibilities: tap, swipe, settings or cancel. Users can choose one of these modalities and close it by staring at the cursor at the left border of the screen. Tap mode will let users click where the cursor is, for example to open another app. In the swipe mode users communicate how much they want to swipe and in which direction they want to move through two taps. The order of the taps run as the swipe of a finger on the screen, so if the first tap is at the upper part and the second at the bottom of the page, it will move downward; while the distance between the two taps indicates the measure of the swipe. More action option lets customers use it in a continuous way, between tap or swipe, until they decide to end it by leaving the cursor at the left border of the screen for a few seconds. Lastly, the cancel mode closes the menu.

The app also allows users to lock the cursor, for example to read something or to give the neck a rest, by moving the cursor on the right border of the screen and holding it still. The cursor also locks itself when a call is made. To activate it again, users will just have to turn the head around in a clockwise motion following the green dots that will appear on the screen. The possibility to call someone without any help is one of the major utilities of the app. It is possible through a tap mode or voice command played by Google saying "Ok Google, call..." and then the name of the person. To end the call users can also activate tap mode and click on the end call button or use just by saying "sesame, end call".

The actual process of developing and launching the app involved two steps. First the "Proof of concept" stage, where they made sure they had all the pieces they needed and that their idea had practical potential. It took a couple of months to fully develop this stage. Then they started to do campaigns to meet up with potential users. The second stage consisted of the actual launching which was done in May 2015. Not only was it successful and had really good user feedback, it also led them to having many partnerships. Google has been a great partner along the way, because of them the development of the app was possible. Through google.org, which is a data-driven, human-focused philanthropy powered by Google, the app became available on their store. They had another local partner (Israel), interested in special needs and together they found people and trained them to distribute over a thousand units.

Ben Dov admits the Sesame app has a long way to go. It was a phone at the beginning which repeatedly crashed during the demo. It was intended for Livne's use at first, but the company also wants it to be available for many other disabilities as stated by Sharon Besser, one of Sesame Enable's investors. She mentions that it is important for them that the device adapts to people who have certain mobility and to those that have little to non-mobility like people in end stages of ALS. In these cases, they would like to adapt it so that it can track eye movements and accommodates to their needs.

The system will have to recognize, for instance, the broad sudden movements of people with cerebral palsy as effectively as the slight, slow movements of people with severe spinal cord injuries. Down the line, Besser says, it will also be important for Sesame Enable to accommodate people with severe ALS, who can't move their heads at all, using vision-tracking technology.

Open sesame offers a great assistance, they have a live chat in their website where it is possible to ask for any kind of question. They also have a FAQ section and tutorial videos, that show all the various uses the app has. It is possible to contact them by mail as well. The invention is now sold in ten states of USA. After a growing partnership with the ALS Association, the company recently moved into new offices within the ALS Association building in Rockville, Maryland. It currently can only be bought on their website and on the android store. It was elected as one of the best apps in the store just recently based on criteria set emphasizing app quality, technical performance, and innovation. For this reason, the main goal is to make smartphones available and reachable to patients with paralysis, spinal cord injury, cerebral palsy, MS, SMD as well as other mobility disabilities. This will help them communicate better and feel included in society.

Open Sesame is a for-profit app, Oded Ben Dov decided it would be for-profit because most of non-profit companies don't survive throughout time. The company started selling it in 1999 as a device but thanks to Google it became an app, available to Android and in a few years to apple, with a more affordable price. The app has a cost of 19.99$ per month. They also have another option which includes a phone or tablet, the app, a lifetime license, and a mounting kit. The prices range from 700$ for the option without the device up to 1800$ for the best option with the mounting kit. The company offers a free one-month trial, to bring people in contact with this revolutionary app, that offers a complete and independent use of their own device.

Open sesame has the ability to create an easier world for people with disabilities. It creates a kind of independence because it permits this forgotten population to use a cell phone and to communicate freely with others. Most of the users are confined to their own beds or wheelchairs, so they now have control over their lives, by making private phone calls independently. Where previously someone had to be present, assisting with dialling or hanging up, users are now able to make their own private calls. This innovation is compatible with other ones, an example, IOT (internet of things) and the app have become an option for controlling one's house environment. But the most important thing is that it also has a positive psychological effect. Users can regain self-esteem and confidence just by the fact that they can use a cell phone like we all do on a daily basis.

Oded, has many good ideas, some of them started as a hobby with a non-profit goal and then became a detailed and developed for-profit project. His first entrepreneurial project is the building of his own company, immediately after graduation. The firm offers app development services in the field of image processing and computer vision. He developed and became proficient in the mastered control of the camera through body movement. During his time at the firm, he developed four Computer Vision apps available on the Play Store. However, the breakthrough took place with the foundation of Sesame Enable in 2012, he created the world's first Touch-free smartphone.

The company started with the development of the "Open Sesame" app but today has launched several products with more functionalities that bring greater accessibility to people with disabilities. The biggest motivation that pushed Oded to the creation of this app was the negligence that affected this sector, underserved and not taken into account. Oded, immediately sought to promote a culture of life that allows people with disabilities to connect, keeping caring for their mental health and being able to use all the features of a smartphone like others do. It is important to consider the passion and the constant commitment that Oded has put in place and continues to put on his inventions, in order to provide the best possible solutions that could better meet the needs of people with disabilities. For Oded, it is very important to make people with disabilities feel included.

4.3.4 Feelif

Visual impairment, generally speaking, is when the ability to correctly see is diminished and can't be fixed with glasses. Blindness is used for patients that have complete or nearly complete vision loss. Such impairment may cause people difficulties in their daily life activities. Blindness is the state or condition of not being able to see due to injury, disease, or a congenital condition; the inability of a person to distinguish darkness from bright light in either eye. It can also be is a severe visual decline in one or both eyes with maintenance of some residual vision. The most common causes of visual impairment are: cataracts, glaucoma, presbyopia, myopia, astigmatism, refractive errors and other visual deficit given by chronic diseases such as diabetes, stroke, corneal clouding, age related macular degeneration, etc.

Željko Khermayer is the innovator of Feelif. When Željko Khermayer was an IT student at the Josef Stefan Institute, he was invited to join a project developing Text-to-Speech software. He realised that blind and visually impaired people could not use Windows and were instead still using DOS. Željko decided to address the issue, by inventing a program called 'Sound Hint' which enabled the blind and visually impaired to use Windows. Although the program was celebrated at conferences and highly appreciated within the community, a lack of funding marked the end of the project. This episode was not enough to stop Željko Khermayer.

About 20 years later, Željko was watching a documentary on the living conditions of deaf-blind people. He was touched, but that's not the emotion he remembers from that night: "I realised that the gap is bigger today than it was back then. So, I decided to change that once again, only this time I wouldn't stop". Željko Khermayer and the

Feelif team developed the first multisensory technology, over 20 multimedia digital apps and the first multisensory smart devices for the blind and visually impaired. His strong motivation brought new opportunities for people with visual loss. In the light of the results, the mission of Željko Khermayer is to empower blind and visually impaired people so that they can easily access information in digital form. He has an outstanding desire to bring digital technology closer to deaf-blind people: dedication and empathy are the main characteristic of this innovator. For that reason, Željko is also a social entrepreneur. His background helped him to be innovative in the healthcare sector: he was CEO of a successful Slovenian digital agency called 4WEB for almost 20 years and he launched an innovative platform called No Payment Portal, which has more than 350K visitors per month.

Current equipment for a blind and visually impaired person is expensive and/or one dimensional. Modern tools are very expensive and rather big to carry around. The Braille display, enables them to feel shapes, but it costs up to EUR 50.000. None of the existing devices allows them to be creative (to draw in digital form, feel shapes, feel drawings, . . .). In addition, playing board games online is difficult and time consuming. Learning with support devices is rather slow, not interactive and not fun. Blind or visually impaired people have problems executing jobs and therefore have difficulties being independent and earning money. One parent (usually mother) is in most cases unemployed or partly employed and care for them. Math teachers usually have problems teaching them how to interpret graphical functions. Social innovation Feelif was developed for so that they could feel shapes and photographs on a standard touch screen. This technology opens new possibilities for them, they can finally use smart devices independently. The technology empowers them through education, own content creation and encourages them to have more creativity.

As mentioned before, Feelif is a multimedia device which allows visual impaired people to feel shapes on a standard touch screen. Feelif is a special app that uses a transparent grid for orientation on the screen surface. A combination of vibrations and voices make the Feelif experience fun. With Feelif a blind person can feel shapes (square, heart etc.), geometric functions, draw, learn Braille, watch interactive stories, express themselves, play games, create content, share/sell/buy content, etc. The device also gives them better access to digital technology. Integration of blind and visually impaired people into the world of sighted and increasing accessibility to digital content is easier with these devices. Moreover, they developed three Feelif devices (Feelif Gamer, Feelif Creator and Feelif Pro) that can play back multisensory digital content.

With Feelif, education and entertainment can be combined. In particular, Feelif devices provide a number of useful tools for blind and visually impaired people to interact with touchscreens and special digital content. It is a tablet made to interact with those who are visually impaired through vibrations. Different elements appear in the screen to interact with them and when the patient moves the fingers around different kinds of vibrations can be felt. Each type of vibration symbolizes a different thing but is also complemented with a speech assistant that helps describe what is being felt as vibrations. Sounds are also used to help assist and describe the figures that appear on the screen. Colors are assigned a specific instrument sound, notes are used to describe directions, realistic natural sounds enforce the scenery description and much more. It is meant to be entertaining and realistic so they can relate with the outer world.

The blind and visually impaired can feel digital content through vibrations, talkback as well as audio and visual information. The multisensory feedback leads to a better, more memorable and more engaging user experience. It is a type of disruptive innovation targeted for the visually impaired. This smart tablet and its added app uses a combination of unique multisensory digital content to make the patient feel more connected to the real world.

Up until now, they are the only providers of multisensory digital content for the blind and visually impaired. To do that, the company works closely with typhlopedagogues, blind and visually impaired and their parents and teachers in order to develop the best content that they actually need. They have developed educational content and digital games for all ages, including chess, four in a row, battleships, memory and more. On top of that, they developed a special application for the teachers and parents of the blind and visually impaired. FeelBook Maker comes pre-installed on the Feelif PRO, and it allows sighted users to create multisensory content for the blind and visually impaired for any Feelif device.

The most important factor to assure the desired is the use of Feelif's Open Platform, that has a purpose of building a community and uniting all stakeholders. It will also be a marketplace for purchasing, selling and sharing Feelif content, which is why the company is also actively working with external developers to produce more content for the blind and visually impaired. Feelif and Feelif Open Platform will help the blind and visually impaired with easier and faster access to the best digital content for them, so they can be more informed, competitive and prepared for life. But not just that: With Feelif and Feelif Open Platform they will have the opportunity to access fun interactive games online. The catchphrase of this company, that synthetize the purpose of this innovation is: "We cannot repair their vision, but surely we can make their lives more interesting, richer and playable. Feelif will have an impact on the quality of their lives."

4WEB and Željko Khermayer developed Feelif, they knew that their technology would help improve the quality of life of blind and visually impaired people. Feelif devices can increase their cognitive capabilities, fine motor skills and spatial awareness, while also acting as a good inclusion tool. At the same time, Feelif technology and Feelif devices can be immensely useful to parents, carers and teachers of blind and visually impaired individuals, as they can easily create content for them. They knew that nobody had created anything like this at the time, and they wanted to take advantage of that.

The innovation process started in 2013, when Željko Khermayer watched a documentary about deaf-blind people and how they live with their disability. Because of their problems with communication and considering that the available technology for communication was expensive and unreachable for most deaf-blind people, he envisioned that smartphones and tablets could be modified to be used by them for everyday activities. By mimicking the pins used in Braille, he was able to distinguish the individual letters of the Braille alphabet. Together with co-workers from the digital firm 4WEB, they developed a special application for touchscreen devices and designed a special relief grid. The concept later became known as Feelif. Throughout the process they worked closely with typhlo pedagogues, the blind and visually impaired community and their parents or caregivers. This was key to understanding their everyday needs.

A couple of visually impaired communities have been their testing partners from the beginning, they would always test their new developments with them and request their feedback. The first concern was whether their technology would work and whether the blind and visually impaired would actually be able to feel shapes with it. After a successful series of rigorous tests and users' feedback the innovation looked very promising. They were very impressed with it and their feedback proved it was immensely useful. A big concern was how to present the innovation abroad and finding a way to get the devices to as many people as possible. The beginning of this social innovation was very exciting, especially when the company realised that they were moving in the right direction. They built a prototype and later received funding from public and private investors. Despite the financial difficulties at the start, when they were reliant on financing from the European Union under the European Regional Development Fund and the Republic of Slovenia, along with private equity funding, they focused on building up their credibility. Having applied to various social innovation and winning some start-up competitions, exciting opportunities came for the company.

Feelif uses several strategies to advertise their product. First of all, they invite users to become ambassadors in order to promote their devices. Moreover, on the website there is a specific part dedicated to the blog where the company publishes information and communication about the value generated by their innovations. They also use social media such as Twitter, Facebook and YouTube which are very widely used nowadays. To build up their credibility and attract the public's attention they exposed their work in an attractive way: in fact, with every award they received, they also received a good amount of media attention. Indeed, Feelif competed and won different national European competitions: communication of the results gave them more market exposure. In 2017, feelif was awarded as the "best European social innovation in Europe". In addition, they have always worked closely with visually impaired communities in Slovenia, who were testing and providing feedback on their devices. Collaborating with different actors, such as institutions, parents, care givers and blind people helped improve the quality of their product and get better the user satisfaction rates. User feedback is useful in making them understand the new unmet needs in order to constantly update their service. It is also helpful for good propaganda when users share their positive experiences while using it.

Values such as inclusion and empowerment have brought many successes to Feelif. With feelif people with visual issues have the possibility to feel included and useful while being independent. Marketing campaigns are now more focused on inclusion and on positive impacts. In addition, Feelif's website has the option to change languages allowing a better commercialization and reach.

Their innovation is widely spread, indeed there are several testimonials that can be found on their website from people all around the world. The company has decided to patent their innovation in order to collect financial resources to sustain the company and to develop new devices. They provide three devices that have different prices and different technical characteristics: *Feelif gamer*: it is a smartphone that costs EUR 699; *Feelif creator*, a tablet that costs EUR 1499; and finally the *Feelif pro*, a new tablet that costs EUR 2499.

It is possible to install several digital games into the Feelif devices from the large library they have available. The company also gives the users the possibility of developing new digital content. These Digital Games for the Blind and Visually Impaired stimulate logical thinking, and are rich in sound effects, music and voice. A special relief grid ensures that the user knows exactly what is happening on the screen and can easily move around it. Entrepreneurial activities/ambition of the innovator (creation of a new firm) and several awards won in innovation field gives us hope that they will continue improving and coming up with innovative ideas. Indeed, Feelif will start to develop an Open Platform: a marketplace used for purchasing, selling and sharing Feelif contents, which is why the company is also actively working with external developers to produce more content for the blind and visually impaired people. Feelif and Feelif Open Platform will help this vulnerable group have easier and faster access to the best digital content online that adapts to their needs. Feelif is a small company, aimed to increase the number of devices and to extend educational content available online. Their business model for Open Platform is still in a drafting stage. Feelif surely gives hope to the blind and visually impaired community.

4.4   Conclusions

Patient innovations are revolutionizing the healthcare industry. More importance is being given to the patient's daily life activities and to the burden a disease or disability can cause them, their social circle, and even the state. Medicine is moving from a paternalistic approach to a two-way communication system. A holistic approach is now being implemented to take into account not only the physical aspect of a patient but also the social, psychological, environmental, etc. Acknowledgement of patient innovations is important in the development and engagement of more patients in health care. Incremental innovation and radical innovation form an important part of the continuous improvement approach of products as well. Having patients, their caregivers or a collaboration of both with other entities is beneficial for the health care market. By developing their own products, they are filling the hole the market has not been able to fill. By reducing these market inefficiencies, they actually help support the system and expose current challenges they face with their ailment. Table 4.2 summarizes the main findings for all the cases here reported.

We think it would be beneficial to include patients that suffer a specific pathology and their caregivers in the process of policy making related to their pathology. Their input is necessary and can even help lower costs or have a more efficient use of resources. Managers of innovation will also be benefited if they decide to include patients in their analysis of the market. Not only does it lower research and development costs but also gives it a more human approach. Listening and comprehending the lives of those affected with specific pathologies makes them feel relatable and makes innovations more personalized and tailored to their every-day needs.

Patient innovation has not been well managed throughout the years and have not been properly diffused. It's because of this that patient innovators have had to handle it with their own hands, with little to no budget and impacting only those close to them or those who are interested and have the means to access their innovations. Hospitals and the state should work together to further encourage PI and to support their ideas when proven to be effective. They should be the bridge between the patient, their ideas and the producers, this way the process will be more legitimate. Patients should feel like the healthcare system in their countries hears and supports them, they should feel included.

The study of 'market needs' can also be diminished if patients and their needs are taken into account. Their contribution to the world is huge and impactful, patient innovations should be praised and acknowledged. Patients are becoming more active and more in control of their diseases. Online patient platforms help them communicate better between each other, share their testimonies, ideas, struggles and successes. The internet should be used to call more innovators and to create committees or groups of support backed up by healthcare organizations to further expand the discussion and development of PI. The state can also help promote UI by doing campaigns and partly or fully financing them in order to open the interest of health care providers and their patients.

We can't deny we are all interconnected with each other even if we live in different continents, in different realities and speak different languages. It's through the internet of things that we can all be one and use this to our advantage. Although mostly only developed countries are now interested in patient innovations and patient engagement; more discovering, encouraging and promotion should be done by healthcare systems in other countries to empower patients. The communities of patients and individuals with complementary skills have great potentials to improve provision of medical care (Zejnilović et al. 2016).

Table 4.2 Case summaries

	Oncomfort	TippyTalk	Open Sesame	Feelif
Innovator	Diane Jooris—Belgian. She has a master's degree in clinical psychology, international relations and laws. Since the diagnosis of both her father and her sister with cancer, Diane decided she wanted to ease the pain experiences her family was going through.	Rob Laffan—Irish. He is a robotic engineer and father of an autistic girl. Rob invented the platform to help his daughter Sadie communicate her emotions, needs and desires.	Oded Ben Dov- Israeli: innovator and fluent speaker of 11 languages, two spoken and nine programming. Giora Liyne (co-founder) an electrical power engineer who became quadriplegic called him to ask him to help him find a way to use his smartphone, to which he accepted.	Željko Khermayer—Slovenian. Željko was watching a documentary on the living conditions of deaf-blind people and the isolation they have because of their condition. He was touched, but that's not the emotion he remembers from that night: "I realised that the gap is bigger today than it was back then. So, I decided to change that once again, only this time I wouldn't stop".
Incumbent technology	Spectacles in which you escape from the real world and are brought to a virtual reality. The distraction of the patient can be done in a Passive or Active way. The systems the company manages are: Aqua, AMO, Kimo, Spacio and Stella.	Before Rob's innovation, some incumbent technologies providing care for such specific illness already existed, but they did not address the ability for a non-verbal person to communicate beyond the boundaries of the room they were present in. Examples of previous ones are: AssistiveWare app, and Tobii Dynavox hardware.	Before the launch of Sesame app in 2012, there was already a similar computer program. This freeware, known as NPointer, is a PC gestural control system that recognizes hand movements and translates them into mouse pointer movements.	Braille has been present for many years but it is limited. Braille Line enables them to read only one line of text. Braille display, enables them to feel shapes, but it costs up to EUR 50.000. Three Feelif devices that can play back multisensory digital content have been made: Feelif Gamer, Feelif Creator and Feelif Pro.
The innovation	Spectacles or goggles with Virtual Reality that can achieve a reduction of anxiety and pain because the attention of the patient is diverted. A person can only give a limited degree of	One-way picture-based communication system, to enable people with verbal disability to instantly connect with anyone, anywhere and anytime. It is a 3-step communicating software:	Android app which enables users to control any app without touching the screen of their smartphones. The device's camera works by tracking the user's head movements. Computer	Feelif is a social innovation developed to improve creativity. It is a multimedia device which allows visual impaired people to feel shapes on a standard touch screen. Feelif is a

	conscious attention to a certain stimulus and experiencing pain demands that conscious attention. The removal of this conscious attention by giving a patient the feeling of being in a different reality ensures that the pain that is felt is less. This reduced feeling of pain therefore causes a reduction in anxiety (Hoffman et al. 2004).	1. Select who you want to talk to, by selecting an image of the person; 2. Select what you want to talk about (by choosing a category and then a specific object); 3. Send the message.	vision algorithms use these movements to create a cursor that appears on the screen of the phone which is controlled by the position and movements of a user's head and even detects minimal movements. The app can be customized, for instance choosing the point sensitivity of the neck movement to control the cursor.	special app plus a transparent grid for orientation on the screen surface. It uses a combination of vibrations and voice raises.
Innovation process	1. Frustration feeling by Diane. 2. Finding solutions 3. Audio solution used but not successful 4. Introduction of virtual reality and partnership with Joowon Kim. 5. Use of virtual reality in cancer patients 6. Extension use in other diagnostic groups.	1. Developing the proof of concept 2. Testing the proof of concept to debug. i.e. making the programmer identify and correct one or more errors (bugs) detected in the software and enhancing performance; 3. Submitting to the Irish patent office, for short-term world-wide patent protection for 2 years; 4. Submitting to the patent office of chosen countries, for full patent protection; 5. Embarking on raising capital and finance; 6. Securing capital and finance; 7. Getting government support; 8. Picking a target market, carefully paying close attention to	1. "Proof of concept", making sure to have all the pieces needed to make it, if the idea had practical potential. It took a couple of months. Then they started meeting potential users. They organized campaigns to meet them. 2. Launching: In May 2015 they launched the first unit. The user feedbacks helped the app become better and better throughout time. They have also had a lot of partnerships.	1. Zeliko watched a documentary about deaf-blind people and simpatized with their isolation and limitations due to their disability. 2. By mimicking the pins used in Braille, he was able to distinguish the individual letters of the Braille alphabet. 3. Development of a special application for touchscreen devices and designing of a special relief grid. 4. Worked closely with visually impaired communities and received feedback. 5. Did testings with visually impaired communities and received feedback. 6. Built a prototype 7. Received funding from

(continued)

Table 4.2 (continued)

	Oncomfort	TippyTalk	Open Sesame	Feelif
		those who need it to talk and communicate; 9. Picking the location; 10. Delivering to the market; 11. Scaling the product to reduce the cost of the app.		public and private investors. 8. Launch of the device.
Communication about the innovation	Widely available in social media.	The first interview for Rob led to a viral video, which got 350 million views, 750.000 shares and 75.000 downloads in just two weeks. The revenue generated from this allowed him to build the TippyTalkEDU (a 2-way communication system)	Widely availably in social media. Official website: https://sesame-enable.com/about-sesame/ The app can only be downloaded in Google Playstore.	They invite users to become ambassadors to promote their devices and can be found in: Twitter, Facebook and YouTube.
Extend of diffusion of innovation and pricing	Oncomfort is based in Brussels, Belgium but is actively engaged in several continents: Europe, North America, South America and Asia. Their software is currently available in eight languages: English, French, Spanish, Portuguese, Italian, German, Arabic and Dutch. The VR therapy is sold to surgeons, anaesthesiologists and any kind of doctor performing anxiety or pain treatments. The VR glasses	TippyTalk is currently used by more than 3500 individuals in more than 50 different countries (84% from the US). TippyTalk is for outside room communication—thus global—providing customized images and costing $100 per year.	After a growing partnership with the ALS Association, the company recently moved into new offices within the ALS Association building in Rockville, Maryland. The app cost per month is: 19.99$. They also have another option which includes a phone or tablet, the app, a lifetime license, and a mounting kit. The price ranges from 700$ for the option without the device, to 1800$ for the	The company has decided to patent their innovation in order to collect financial resources to sustain the company and to develop new devices. The company provides three devices that have different prices and different technical characteristics: • Feelif game: a smartphone that costs EUR 699; • Feelif creator: a tablet that costs EUR 1499;

are sold for 740 euro a piece, without generating any profit to Oncomfort.	option with the mounting kit. The company offers a free one-month trial.		• Feelid pro: a new tablet that costs EUR 2499.
Entrepreneurial activities/ambition of the innovator	On comfort wants to enter the mental health medical area and would like that in the future doctors could prescribe VR as a type of anxiety treatment. They would also like to be part of the whole cancer journey from diagnosis to treatment and beyond.	Open Sesame was first sold in 1999 as a device but thanks to Google it became an app, available to Androids and in a few years hopefully to Apple devices. His firm offers app development services in the field of image processing and computer vision.	TippyTalk's next goal is that of applying and introducing their product into the K12 special needs school districts of the US and hopefully worldwide.	Željko Khermayer and the Feelif team have developed the first multisensory technology, over 20 multimedia digital apps and the first multisensory smart devices for the blind and visually impaired. The mission of Željko Khermayer is to empower blind and visually impaired people so that they can easily access information in a digital form. The company also gives the users the possibility of developing new digital content.

Source: Adapted by the author

References

Al-Khotani, A., Bello, L. A. A., & Christidis, N. (2016). Effects of audiovisual distraction on children's behaviour during dental treatment: A randomized controlled clinical trial. *Acta Odontologica Scandinavica, 74*(6), 494–501.

Aminabadi, N. A., Erfanparast, L., Sohrabi, A., Oskouei, S. G., & Naghili, A. (2012). The impact of virtual reality distraction on pain and anxiety during dental treatment in 4-6 year-old children: A randomized controlled clinical trial. *Journal of Dental Research, Dental Clinics, Dental Prospects, 6*(4), 117.

Bray, F., Ferlay, J., Soerjomataram, I., Siegel, R. L., Torre, L. A., & Jemal, A. (2018). Global cancer statistics 2018: GLOBOCAN estimates of incidence and mortality worldwide for 36 cancers in 185 countries. *CA: A Cancer Journal for Clinicians, 68*(6), 394–424.

Cherny, N., Ripamonti, C., Pereira, J., Davis, C., Fallon, M., McQuay, H., & Expert Working Group of the European Association of Palliative Care Network. (2001). Strategies to manage the adverse effects of oral morphine: An evidence-based report. *Journal of Clinical Oncology, 19* (9), 2542–2554.

Ebrahimi, H., Namdar, H., Ghahramanpour, M., Ghafourifard, M., & Musavi, S. (2018). Effect of virtual reality method and multimedia system on burn patients' pain during dressing. *Journal of Clinical and Analytical Medicine, 6*(4), 54–61.

Guarino, D., La Paglia, F., Daino, M., Maiorca, V., Zichichi, S., Guccione, F., & La Barbera, D. (2017). Chronic pain treatment through virtual reality. *Annual Review of Cybertherapy and Telemedicine, 15*, 181–184.

Guo, C., Deng, H., & Yang, J. (2015). Effect of virtual reality distraction on pain among patients with hand injury undergoing dressing change. *Journal of Clinical Nursing, 24*(1–2), 115–120.

Hoffman, H. G., Sharar, S. R., Coda, B., Everett, J. J., Ciol, M., Richards, T., & Patterson, D. R. (2004). Manipulating presence influences the magnitude of virtual reality analgesia. *Pain, 111* (1–2), 162–168.

Hoffman, H. G., Seibel, E. J., Richards, T. L., Furness, T. A., Patterson, D. R., & Sharar, S. R. (2006). Virtual reality helmet display quality influences the magnitude of virtual reality analgesia. *The Journal of Pain, 7*(11), 843–850.

Kindler, C. H., Harms, C., Amsler, F., Ihde-Scholl, T., & Scheidegger, D. (2000). The visual analog scale allows effective measurement of preoperative anxiety and detection of patients' anesthetic concerns. *Anesthesia & Analgesia, 90*(3), 706–712.

Mavridou, P., Dimitriou, V., Manataki, A., Arnaoutoglou, E., & Papadopoulos, G. (2013). Patient's anxiety and fear of anesthesia: Effect of gender, age, education, and previous experience of anesthesia. A survey of 400 patients. *Journal of Anesthesia, 27*(1), 104–108.

Mayo Clinic Staff. Cancer. October 4 2018. Mayo Clinic. Retrieved from https://www.mayoclinic.org/diseases-conditions/cancer/symptoms-causes/syc-20370588

Miles, M. B., Huberman, A. M., Huberman, M. A., & Huberman, M. (1994). *Qualitative data analysis: An expanded sourcebook.* Thousand Oaks, CA: Sage.

Miloff, A., Lindner, P., Hamilton, W., Reuterskiöld, L., Andersson, G., & Carlbring, P. (2016). Single-session gamified virtual reality exposure therapy for spider phobia vs. traditional exposure therapy: Study protocol for a randomized controlled non-inferiority trial. *Trials, 17*(1), 60.

National Center for Health Statistics. (2006). *Health, United States, 2006 with chartbook on trends in the health of Americans.* Hyattsville, MD.

National Cancer Institute (2012). *Psychological stress and cancer.* Retrieved from https://www.cancer.gov/about-cancer/coping/feelings/stress-fact-sheet

Nilsson, S., Finnström, B., Kokinsky, E., & Enskär, K. (2009). The use of virtual reality for needle-related procedural pain and distress in children and adolescents in a paediatric oncology unit. *European Journal of Oncology Nursing, 13*(2), 102–109.

Oncomfort (2017). *Digital sedation.* Retrieved from https://www.oncomfort.com/en/

Pandya, P. G., Kim, T. E., Howard, S. K., Stary, E., Leng, J. C., Hunter, O. O., & Mariano, E. R. (2017). Virtual reality distraction decreases routine intravenous sedation and procedure-related pain during preoperative adductor canal catheter insertion: A retrospective study. *Korean Journal of Anesthesiology, 70*(4), 439–445.

Pourmand, A., Davis, S., Marchak, A., Whiteside, T., & Sikka, N. (2018). Virtual reality as a clinical tool for pain management. *Current Pain and Headache Reports, 22*(8), 53.

Prabhakar, A. R., Marwah, N., & Raju, O. S. (2007). A comparison between audio and audiovisual distraction techniques in managing anxious pediatric dental patients. *Journal of Indian Society of Pedodontics and Preventive Dentistry, 25*(4), 177.

Psychological Stress and Cancer. National Cancer Institute. NIH. December 2012. Retrieved from https://www.cancer.gov/about-cancer/coping/feelings/stress-fact-sheet

Ramamohan, D., Indira, S., Sateesh, S., Kumar, S. S., Bhandarkar, P., Bhat, N. S., & Agrawal, A. (2018). Understanding preoperative anxiety in patients before elective surgical intervention. *International Journal of Academic Medicine, 4*(1), 56.

Remes, O., Wainwright, N., Surtees, P., Lafortune, L., Khaw, K. T., & Brayne, C. (2018). Generalised anxiety disorder and hospital admissions: Findings from a large, population cohort study. *BMJ Open, 8*(10), e018539.

Schmitt, Y. S., Hoffman, H. G., Blough, D. K., Patterson, D. R., Jensen, M. P., Soltani, M., & Sharar, S. R. (2011). A randomized, controlled trial of immersive virtual reality analgesia, during physical therapy for pediatric burns. *Burns, 37*(1), 61–68.

Stake, R. E. (2005). Qualitative case studies. In N. K. Denzin & Y. S. Lincoln (Eds.), *The Sage handbook of qualitative research* (pp. 443–466). Thousand Oaks, CA: Sage.

Tanja-Dijkstra, K., Pahl, S., White, M. P., Auvray, M., Stone, R. J., Andrade, J., & Moles, D. R. (2018). The Soothing sea: A virtual coastal walk can reduce experienced and recollected pain. *Environment and Behavior, 50*(6), 599–625.

Van Steenkist, M. (2018). Belgische start-up wil narcose vervangen door virtual reality. *Knack.* Retrieved from https://datanews.knack.be/ict/start-ups/belgische-start-up-wil-narcose-vervangen-door-virtual-reality/article-normal-1184237.html?cookie_check=1544109602

Yin, R. K. (2009). *Case study research: Design and methods* (4th ed.). Thousand Oaks, CA: Sage.

Zejnilović, L., Oliveira, P., & Canhão, H. (2016). Innovations by and for patients, and their place in the future health care system. In *Boundaryless hospital* (pp. 341–357). Berlin, Heidelberg: Springer.

Printed in the United States
By Bookmasters